There is no greater love than this,
that a man should lay down his life for his friends.

—*John 15:13–14, New Testament*

KILL FOR THRILL

THE CRIME SPREE THAT ROCKED WESTERN PENNSYLVANIA

MICHAEL SHEETZ

THE History PRESS

Published by The History Press
Charleston, SC 29403
www.historypress.net

First published 2009
Second printing 2009

Manufactured in the United States

ISBN 978.1.59629.498.1

Library of Congress Cataloging-in-Publication Data

Sheetz, Michael.
Kill for thrill : the crime spree that rocked western Pennsylvania /
Michael W. Sheetz.
p. cm.
ISBN 978-1-59629-498-1
1. Serial murders--Pennsylvania--Case studies. 2. Serial murderers--Pennsylvania--Case studies. 3. Serial murder investigation--Pennsylvania--Case studies. I. Title.
HV6533.P4S54 2009
364.152'3209227488--dc22
2009000032

In memory of those who have fallen.

Contents

Preface	9
Acknowledgements	13
Introduction	15
PART I	
In Which the Scene Is Set	21
Leonard Miller, Model Public Servant	25
John Lesko and His Wretched Existence	29
Peter Levato Becomes the First Victim	35
PART II	
Edward Wolak Finds the Body	41
Meet Michael Travaglia	45
The Case of the Stolen Kielbasa	51
Marlene Sue Newcomer Becomes the Second Victim	58
PART III	
Sergeant Tridico Connects the Dots	65
Bill Nicholls Becomes the Third Victim	70
The Fourth Victim Is Claimed	76
Sergeant Tridico Vows to Find the Killers	82

CONTENTS

PART IV

The Search Is On 87

Doggone Sam's 91

Travaglia and Lesko Are Apprehended 95

Epilogue 99

Afterword 103

Appendix 105

Preface

The story you are about to read is true. Not true as in "based on," not true as in "inspired by," but true as in these events actually happened to real people, in real places and in actual history. To the extent possible, I have culled every detail of this book from original sources—no mean feat considering that many of the events are rapidly approaching their thirtieth anniversary. This work is nonfiction and all events are true; however, in parts I have taken storytelling liberties. In particular, where people and witnesses are no longer available or memories have faded, I have provided my best interpretation of what most likely happened or was said, based on my years of research, interviews, trial transcripts, forensic evidence and firsthand accounts of the incidents by witnesses. Where the story strays from strict nonfiction, I have nonetheless remained true to the factual events as they unfolded.

While I have paid scrupulous attention to detail, you should be aware that, where the ravages of time and circumstance demand, gaps in verifiable information have been filled in with reasonable extrapolations of what is likely to have happened. When this happens, rest assured that any detail not verifiable with underlying source documentation has absolutely no material bearing on this account. Instead, it merely serves, in the few places that it occurs, to add readability to this tale.

As in everyday life, factual accounts often differ in trivial ways. In the event that my research has unearthed conflicting versions or diverging accounts of an event, I have attempted to identify the most reasonable alternative and have made every effort to provide authentic accounts of every material detail.

While researching this story, I attempted to contact the accused. Sadly, these attempts were fruitless, and for whatever reason, they chose not to add their perspectives to the book.

In addition, I have corresponded with many of the people whose lives this story has touched. Some have died, some have moved away and are unreachable and others have, for personal reasons, chosen to decline my request for an interview. I have attempted as much as possible to respect the privacy of those families of victims who wish to remain in the wings and have endeavored to treat the circumstances surrounding their loved ones' deaths with accuracy and dignity.

The brevity of the period that these events cover belies the far-reaching and monstrous effect they have had on the lives of so many innocent people. Police officers such as Donald Mahan, Robin Davis, Jim Clawson and Thomas Tridico will forever carry the heavy burden of losing a fellow officer. Likewise, the family and friends of Michael Travaglia and John Lesko's other victims can never truly put behind them the dreadful events that took their loved ones from them.

In some ways, even the passage of twenty-nine years cannot dull the ache that still permeates the pastoral rolling hills that surround Pittsburgh. This is true in part because while the courts convicted Travaglia and Lesko of these murders over twenty-eight years ago, they remain two of America's most senior death row inmates. Some say that this is an injustice that is unconscionable in our society.

Since their original conviction in 1981, appeals that Michael Travaglia and John Lesko have pursued have traversed their way up and down Pennsylvania's court system. As you are about to read, hearings, trial, retrials and resentencings have come and gone, and both men have had death warrants signed—and stayed—twice. Yet they both remain on their respective death rows while friends and loved ones of their victims are left wondering, what is the price of justice?

Death penalty ideologies notwithstanding, loved ones who have suffered double victimization, first at the hands of the defendants and second at the hands of the system, cannot achieve closure and begin the healing process until the final chapter of this story is written. It is a chapter that, despite all of my hoping and scheming, I am unable to create. If this were a work of fiction, I would have already written a blockbuster ending. Sadly, it is not.

Preface

Beyond mere curiosity, this project has been cathartic in a way. I also have been touched by the events you are about to read. I grew up ten minutes from the very spot where Leonard Miller's body fell. I went to the same high school as Michael J. Travaglia. In fact, in 1984, a mere four years after Leonard Miller was brutally murdered, I walked the same station house hallways, wore the same uniform patch and patrolled the same city streets that Leonard once patrolled.

I never met Leonard, but colleagues such as the late Rick Murphy, chief of police at the time Leonard was murdered, and Jim Clawson, chief during my tenure, have shared with me insights into what measure of man Leonard Miller was. I had the opportunity to work with Rick Murphy for several years before his death in 1997. He was kind enough to share insight about Leonard Miller the officer—and the man. I am indebted. You will read of Leonard Miller in the coming chapters. I hope that I have done justice to his memory.

However, this book is not just about Leonard Miller. Sometimes we are swept away by the atrocity and senselessness of acts that are beyond our comprehension. The murder of a police officer is such an act. However, Leonard's murder was only the final coup de grâce in a weeklong nightmare that took the lives of three other innocent victims, who, but for the happenstance of fate, could have just as easily been reading about these events instead of being involved in them.

In the coming chapters you will meet them all. Marlene Sue Newcomer was a seamstress and mother. Peter Levato was a down-on-his-luck security guard. William Nicholls was a loving son, brother and devoted member of his local church parish. Similar to all of us, they were human beings with human stories. They came from different backgrounds and had different lives. They are all, however, inseparably bound together by one inescapable fact—they encountered Michael Travaglia and John Lesko at the height of their depravity. You will read the facts of their lives as we know them, you will learn of the dreadful fates that befell them and through it all you will ask yourself, why did this happen?

Thanks to the tireless efforts of Sergeant Thomas Tridico (retired) and his fellow troopers of the Pennsylvania State Police, there have been few aspects of this case left open to speculation. The trial testimony of witnesses, the forensic evidence and even the chilling statements of the defendants themselves have answered many of our questions. Some, however, remain.

Investigators, victims' families and the thousands of residents of the quiet valleys surrounding Pittsburgh search to this day for words to explain what caused two men to snap in such a horrific, violent and unpredictable way. The carnage they left behind still haunts those closest to it.

As we look back at the lives of Michael Travaglia and John Lesko, we will see two men who are in many ways similar yet, in others, wildly different. These are men who, for the most part, led uneventful lives; lives of mediocrity. Individually, they are indistinct and innocuous. However, each found in the other some indefinable and undeniable element that united them in a relentless pursuit of violence and depravity.

Perhaps the nonstop drug and alcohol abuse that punctuated that infamous week destroyed their abilities to think rationally. Perhaps, as some have claimed, John Lesko was defective and his latent homophobic rage boiled over into a murderous rampage. Alternatively, perhaps there is no truly rational reason. After all, some actions seem to defy explanation and refuse to comply with our very human need to neatly compartmentalize everything in our world.

We may never unravel the why. Instead, what follows is a factual account of the events of those eight days.

Acknowledgements

A project of the scope of *Kill for Thrill* would not have been possible had it not been for the tremendous support that I received from so many people. From the research and investigation stage to the conceptualization stage to the editorial stage, I am indebted to so many people that I cannot possibly repay them for their untiring support. If I were to list everyone whose contributions to this project made it possible, the acknowledgements section would far exceed the length of the entire book. However, there are several people in particular whose close associations with the project have made it far more manageable:

Thomas Tridico, who has offered me insight, shared his experiences and provided me with details that otherwise would have gone unrecorded in history.

Dr. William H. Kerr, who was instrumental in bringing greater personal perspective to the events of Christmas 1979 and was kind enough to share with me many of his personal writings and ruminations on the murder of Leonard Miller.

Jim Clawson, who was perhaps Leonard's closest friend at the time of his death. By graciously allowing me into his world, Jim offered me a very precious glance of who Leonard Miller was.

Dr. Maggie Patterson, professor of communications at Duquesne University, who was tremendously helpful in understanding the events that made John Lesko the person he is. Her research and that of her students into John Lesko and his family have formed the basis for much of what ends up being a very shocking glimpse of what it must have been like to be John Lesko in 1979.

Rick Facchine, with whom I worked during most of my police career. I am permanently in his debt. He acted as a visionary, a sounding board, an instigator and, above all, a good friend during twenty years of policing and beyond.

The late Richard Murphy, who will never know how helpful his sardonic wit and down-to-earth manner were in helping me understand Leonard Miller a little bit better.

For their tireless editorial support, I would like to thank my mother and father, Ronald Sheetz and Carol Sue Nichols, and my wife, Susan, whose patience gave me the courage to finish this project.

Introduction

Although this book is intentionally neutral on the validity or efficacy of the death penalty as a means of punishment for criminal conduct, the implication of everything that it touches nearly screams for attention.

Like any emotionally charged topic, death penalty discussions often create strong division among its various factions. In this matter, there are rarely abstainers from the debate, and usually both camps offer strong, emotion-laden defenses of their positions.

In this brief introduction, you will hear neither emotion nor argument. Instead, what I have prepared for you is a cursory overview of the death penalty that may await Travaglia and Lesko at the end of this completely sordid ordeal.

In November 1990, Governor Robert P. Casey signed into law a bill changing Pennsylvania's method of execution from death by electrocution to death by lethal injection. For many years, the state kept the methods, exact drugs composing the lethal cocktail and execution procedures strictly confidential. However, recent disclosures by the state have made the execution process more transparent.

Pursuant to the switch to lethal injection, Pennsylvania dismantled its electric chair and, in 1997, remodeled the execution complex at SCI Rockview. As part of the renovations, the state relocated the complex to a former field hospital on the grounds of the facility but outside the walls of the prison. Included in the complex, in addition to the execution chamber itself, are three maximum-security cells used to house condemned inmates immediately before the state carries out their sentences, office space and the apparatus of the execution.

The new location of the complex offers several benefits to corrections officials, including easing the preparation process without disturbing the day-to-day operations of the rest of the facility. Additionally, it allows the witnesses and family members to attend the execution without having to pass into the facility. Officials herald this as an increase in safety and security.

While the execution complex is used to house condemned inmates immediately prior to their execution, inmates under a pending sentence of death are housed in administrative custody status in a housing area known as Restricted Housing Units (RHU). Even though Pennsylvania has several maximum-security facilities, currently the only facilities that Pennsylvania state law authorizes to house death row inmates are State Correctional Institutes (SCI) Greene and Graterford for men and SCI Muncy for women.

Once the governor has signed the condemned inmate's death warrant, officials transfer him to solitary confinement, where he is under constant direct supervision. His visitation rights are also severely restricted. In most circumstances, immediate family, legal counsel and a designated member of the clergy are the only people who may visit the inmate.

In addition to restrictions on their visitation, inmates' personal belongings are strictly limited. Guards allow them a mattress, a pillow, a blanket, sheets, a towel, a bar of soap, their institutional clothing, some limited religious material, legal papers, a few personal photos and very few consumables like cigarettes, a toothbrush, toothpaste and pens/pencils. In addition, an inmate may possess one book at a time and may have a television or radio placed outside his cell and within view for a limited time each day.

On the day prior to the execution, the inmate is prepared for execution and offered a selection of a last meal from a prepared list of available items. Contrary to Hollywood portrayals, the prisoner's last meal is not anything he chooses. Instead, each inmate is given a list of available meals from which to choose his final meal.

At the designated time of execution, the execution team escorts the inmate to the injection room, where team members strap him to a gurney. One intravenous needle is then inserted into each arm—one primary to carry out the execution and a backup in the event that the first fails to perform properly. The tubes from these IV needles are connected to an IV pump in another room, and a saline drip is begun to ensure proper flow of liquids into the prisoner's system.

Medical personnel attach a heart monitor to the inmate, and once the execution team receives confirmation from the warden that the execution is to proceed, someone opens the curtain separating the injection room from the observation gallery. Once the defendant has completed his final words, the warden signals that the execution is to begin. Barring a last-minute stay, the execution team begins to administer a lethal cocktail of drugs consisting of two to five grams of sodium thiopental (commonly known as sodium pentothal), one hundred milligrams of pancuronium bromide and one hundred microequivalents of potassium chloride.

Sodium thiopental is an ultra–short acting barbiturate, which in high dosages causes near instantaneous coma. At nearly five times the average normal dose, the amount used in the execution cocktail is usually sufficient to induce coma within ten seconds.

Pancuronium bromide acts as a paralyzing agent, inducing total muscular paralysis within fifteen to thirty seconds. Although some states use tubocurarine chloride or succinylcholine chloride, they all serve the same function in the execution cocktail—paralyze the defendant and induce respiratory arrest within thirty seconds.

Between the delivery of each drug in the cocktail, technicians flush the IV lines in order to prevent accidental mixtures of the three drugs. Inadvertent mixing of the chemicals would form precipitates and would ultimately block the tubing, leading to a botched execution.

The final drug in the cocktail is one hundred microequivalents of potassium chloride. Potassium chloride is an electrolyte. It elevates the levels of potassium in the system, which interfere with the ability of the heart muscle to contract. With the amount of potassium chloride in the execution cocktail, onset of cardiac arrest is quite rapid, irreversible and fatal.

While the execution team administers the cocktail, medical personnel continuously monitor the inmate's heart rate until all cardiac activity has stopped. Once the attending physician makes a pronouncement of death, the warden declares the inmate a "Phase III" inmate and the execution is completed. During the execution, death commonly occurs within seven minutes of the first drug entering the inmate's system.

Regardless of your personal stance, individual outlook or jurisprudential viewpoint, the questions raised in the name of due process, fairness and proportionality ring truer for the death penalty than for anywhere else in our criminal justice system. In the words of Justice Sutherland, when speaking of the government's obligation to ensure fairness:

> *The United States Attorney is a representative not of an ordinary party to a controversy, but of a sovereignty whose obligation to govern impartially is as compelling as its obligation to govern at all; and whose interest therefore in a criminal prosecution is not that it shall win a case, but that justice shall be done…He may prosecute with earnestness and vigor—indeed he should do so. But, while he may strike hard blows, he is not at liberty to strike foul ones. It is as much his duty to refrain from improper methods calculated to produce a wrongful conviction, as it is to use every legitimate means to bring about a just one.*

While the prosecutorial conduct in the Lesko and Travaglia case is beyond reproach, the significance and gravity of the task that the government has been asked to undertake in this case serves not just as a reminder of the need for due process in this particular case, but also as a cautionary tale directed at the entire system, and as Justice Sutherland opined, it is the duty of those charged by the people with protecting the people to ensure that it is justice, not vengeance and not winning, that carries the day.

As the Travaglia and Lesko case unfolds, the somber reminder of this introduction should inform your reading. Understand well that at the end of the day, two men, deserving of society's harshest punishment no doubt, will be strapped to a gurney, and with methodical, calculated precision, representatives of the larger society will legally and justifiably end their lives. Deserving of death or otherwise, there is no retrenchment from this punishment. Death is permanent, and given its permanence, extreme safeguards are called for.

What is left for others to decide—because this book will not attempt to do so—is at what point do we draw the line? Where shall we say enough is enough? Will we draw that line at some arbitrary point—say, four appeals? Alternatively, will we manage it on a case-by-case basis, evaluating every circumstance in order to say that we are certain beyond equivocation that we have made no mistakes? Have we, in fact, sent the proper man to his death for the proper reasons? The answers to these questions are not in the pages of this book—nor would I speculate are they in the pages of any book. Instead, they live inside each of us as we make decisions about what society owes its individuals—the innocent as well as the accused.

What *is* in this book are facts. Facts that, when taken together, paint a picture of dozens of lives irreparably broken due to the violent and depraved actions of two young men. These two men ripped parents and children from their loved ones. Communities were torn apart as they laid to rest their sons and daughters before their time. Two men whom you will grow to know intimately—men who, as of 2008, still sit on death row, unrepentant and unashamed—visited all of this repugnance within an eight-day period. Balance their lives against the lives of four innocent human beings who, if for no other reason, died because they were in the wrong place at the wrong time. In the end, you will have to decide for yourself what the fitting end to the story is because, as you will see, I cannot.

Part I

In Which the Scene Is Set

Leonard Miller pulled the heavy wooden door closed behind him and began the short walk to the back door of the station house. There were twenty steps to the door. Leonard only needed fifteen lumbering strides. At six feet, two inches tall, Leonard's broad shoulders seemed to scrape the pale green walls as he strolled down the hall.

As he reached the end of the hallway, he thrust the heavy red door outward and stepped onto the sidewalk. Zipping his police jacket, he instinctively checked up and down the street. Lonely. Silent. Dark. As usual, North Pennsylvania Avenue was as deserted as the rest of Apollo Borough. At three o'clock in the morning, two days after New Years, it was even more so.

Nestled along the banks of the shallow, meandering Kiskiminetas River, for many years the tiny town of Apollo, Pennsylvania, had been home to the countless workers who commuted daily to and from the foundries and steel mills that once made Pittsburgh and its surrounding hills the epicenter of the Industrial Revolution. This one-square-mile flyspeck, caught between the river and the rural pasturelands of the rest of Armstrong County, was in serious economic decline. Just like every other mill town, Apollo had begun to give ground in its battle against the economic decline that had set upon the steel valley in the mid- to late 1970s. It was in this struggling community that Leonard Miller had made his mark and reached his dream.

As Leonard wedged his 250-pound frame behind the wheel of his black-and-white Chevy Nova, the light from the streetlamp bouncing off the silver shield on his left breast caught his attention and filled him with satisfaction at how far his journey had brought him. Although this was only Leonard's third day as a full-time police officer, he knew these quiet streets backward and forward. After patrolling them for nearly three years, he was living his lifelong dream.

He pulled the seatbelt across his lap, adjusted it to fit his ample chest and then scribbled down his starting mileage. Once he had slipped his pen into the shiny black pocket of his jacket, he dropped the Nova into gear, pulled onto deserted Pennsylvania Avenue and then headed toward "downtown" Apollo.

When he rode past the fire hall, Leonard glanced instinctively at the gleaming white engines of the Apollo Volunteer Fire Department that were peeking out at him from the windows of their warm home. He knew these engines well. Two short blocks and one left turn later, he was heading down First Street toward North Plaza, the heart of the town's tiny business district.

Leonard swung into the alley behind Armitages hardware store. He killed the headlights and slowed the cruiser to a crawl. The alley was inky black, so it took him a few moments before his eyes adjusted. Slowly, the shadows and blobs of the alley began to take shape. He began to survey the rear entrances to the businesses that lined the east end of the plaza. Adjusting the angle of the car's Visibeam spotlight, he flipped the switch, instantly drenching the alley in ten thousand candlepower of light. Too cold for either man or beast, the alley was as he had hoped—empty. He doused the light and then inched along toward Grove Street.

At the intersection, he looked left and right and then made a cautious left turn onto Grove.

Michael Travaglia gripped the wheel of the Fiat Lancia tightly as he flew toward Apollo. His boney knuckles were white with anticipation. In the passenger's seat, John Lesko pulled a .22-caliber revolver from the waistband of his pants, fiddled with the cylinder and then, obviously reassured, slid the six-inch barrel back into his greasy bluejeans.

In the backseat, fifteen-year-old Ricky Rutherford sat riveted, eyes fixed on the centerline of the highway as it sped past. Ricky had joined Michael and John only one day before. Tonight was a night that he would regret for the rest of his life. Coolly, John glanced at Michael, "Where are we headed?"

"We need money, right? I know of a perfect place just up the road." Zipping past Hancock Avenue and around the gently curving highway, the three men rode in silent, unspoken agreement, each anticipating their approaching adventure.

Leonard pulled into North Plaza and parked his car. Bracing for the cold, he turned up the black fur collar of his jacket and stepped onto the gray parking lot. The sound of the slamming car door bounced off the washed-out clapboard siding of the sleeping Chambers Hotel and then echoed down Warren Avenue. He mashed the button on his Kelight and then readjusted his collar so that the back brim of his round, felt, Smokey the Bear–style hat was nestled tightly against the back of his collar. He hated the hat, yet for the little warmth it could provide, he would wear it anyway. He tucked his neck down into his jacket like a turtle and set out toward the bank.

Taking a tactical approach to the giant glass façade of the Apollo Community Trust, Leonard flicked the light back and forth inside the lobby until he was satisfied that it was empty. He took two giant steps up to the door and gave it a quick tug—rock solid, just as he had hoped. He glanced at his watch—4:36 in the morning. Only three and a half hours until he was home, warm in his bed. All Leonard Miller wanted on that subzero January night was to get to the end of his shift and curl up under the warm blankets in his own bed.

Leonard crossed west on Warren Avenue and for good measure rattled the doors of the pharmacy—still no signs of life or mischief. Reassured that all was well in Apollo Borough, Leonard briskly pushed his way through the cutting wind that scuttled across the plaza parking lot and made his way toward the relative warmth of his waiting cruiser. Once he was again safely situated behind the wheel, he fired up the 350-cubic-inch police interceptor engine and headed toward the only oasis in the vast midnight wasteland—the Stop-N-Go.

On the southwest end of the plaza, two lonely cars snoozed in stalls in front of the Stop-N-Go. Luminescent warm light spilled out of the tiny store onto the sidewalk, inviting Leonard inside. Linda McLaughlin and Thomas Bodnar had already sought refuge from the chilling winds and hovered over two steaming cups of syrupy convenience store coffee. Leonard slipped his car in beside the others and quickly joined them inside.

To the north, the glow of city lights inched above the horizon. Michael sensed the nearness of his quest and goosed the sports car along. As he stared down at the yellow line, his thin lips curved into an evil smile at the thought of another robbery. The headlights pierced the darkness, quickly eating up miles of salt-stained highway. As they roared closer and closer to Apollo, the tension in the car rose to a palpable level. It made each gentle curve in the highway feel as if it were the hairpin of Monte Carlo. Then, almost as if Michael had willed it, the bridge appeared in front of them.

The Apollo Bridge stretches fewer than 150 yards across the shallow Kiskiminetas River. It is the dividing line between Westmoreland County to the west and Armstrong County and the borough of Apollo to the east. The metal grating that covered its deck made a distinctive *hum-thrumming* sound as the Lancia skimmed across. Then the sound caromed off Patrick's Pub and ricocheted down into the valley to die.

As the trio emerged from the east end of the bridge, their thoughts of a quick score at the Stop-N-Go faded quickly. Spotting the police car parked in front of the store, Michael quickly came up with a solution to the dilemma. "I want to have some fun with this cop," he announced to his partners, and he gunned the Lancia, willing the speedometer higher. He sped past the store and then roared up First Street, heading toward Apollo-Ridge High School.

By the time the Lancia topped the hill heading out of town toward Spring Church, it was obvious that the cop had not pursued them. Michael felt the burn of angry bile in the back of his throat.

"Let it go Mike," Ricky said.

"F--- no. We're gonna get this guy to chase us and then go back and knock off that store." Michael skidded the car off the highway, hung a sharp U-turn and quickly pulled back out onto First Street headed back into town. They were going to rob that store. He wouldn't back down this time. The tiny sports car lurched forward like a gunshot.

As the darkened homes began to zip by faster and faster, the blood seemed to drain from Ricky's face. Over the hill, down into town and through the intersection of Pennsylvania Avenue the Lancia flew at close to eighty miles an hour. When the lights of the Stop-N-Go appeared, Michael began blowing the horn. This time, that cop would chase them—he wouldn't have it any other way. Michael smiled.

The car flew past the plaza and toward the bridge, and then, as they passed through the intersection, brilliant blue and red flashes ruptured the night air. Glancing in the mirror, Michael could see the piercing headlights of the police cruiser as it pulled out of the plaza onto First Street in full pursuit mode. Pushing the throttle harder, he sped back onto the bridge heading into Westmoreland County.

Ricky Rutherford looked nauseated and scared. He glanced first at Michael and then at John. As the tiny car rocketed across the bridge, John Lesko turned in his seat, leaned toward Ricky and said, "Lay down in the back. This is gonna turn into a shooting gallery."

LEONARD MILLER, MODEL PUBLIC SERVANT

On January 3, 1980, Leonard Miller had donned badge #78 for only the third time as a full-time patrol officer; however, those three short days belie the level of community pride and commitment to public service that filled his spirit. For as long as friends and relatives could recall, Leonard Miller had been determined to be a cop. From the age of four onward, it was all that he ever wanted to do. It was a calling that had consumed him and had driven him to become an active volunteer in all aspects of his community.

Whether serving as an emergency medical technician, volunteer firefighter for the Kiski Township Fire Department or as a member of the local emergency dispatch services' emergency response team, Leonard Miller's heart and soul were always his service to the community.

Through it all, Evelyn and Frank Miller had always supported their son's desire to serve, but they had mixed feelings about his dream of becoming a police officer. Even though both wholeheartedly backed Leonard's ambitions and dreams, they worried, as parents do, about Leonard's safety. Police work is dangerous—even in the sleepy coal-patch towns along the rivers of western Pennsylvania. Long hours, low pay and danger were all factors that Evelyn and Frank had accepted as they proudly encouraged their son to pursue his dream. Leonard knew the dangers as well, and yet he was undaunted. Even though Leonard's dream was to become a police officer, the economy and the troubled times of the late 1970s had conspired against him.

In 1979, Apollo, Pennsylvania, was a typical rural, western Pennsylvania town. Apart from the dual distinctions of being the only U.S. town to share the name of a lunar spacecraft and being one of only a handful of towns whose names are palindromes, there was little to distinguish it from the dozens of other dying boroughs and villages sprawled along the meandering Kiskiminetas River.

Born of coal and steel, western Pennsylvania's economy suffered tremendous hardships during the mid- to late 1970s. Caused partly by the collapse of big steel and partly by the generally sluggish economic times that had begun to grip the nation, this economic decline took its toll on Apollo. In this valley, employment in one of the literally dozens of steel mills that littered the rivers of the steel city was de rigueur for nearly everyone. Quickly, these steel towns began to collapse under the weight of growing unemployment and the declining dollar.

With the economic decay that swept across the rust belt came a reduced tax base. With a reduced tax base, cities and towns inevitably began cutting costs and tightening belts. Making the fiscal ends meet is a difficult job in good economic times—declining economic conditions made that task even more difficult.

As with any business, the cost of labor is one of a city's greatest expenditures and one of the first places town fathers began to look when trying to trim budgets and make ends meet. Town councils, mayors and tax collectors faced this exact predicament during the 1970s in rural western Pennsylvania.

Throughout the Alle-Kiski Valley, city services continued to be a high priority; however, town councils dealt with them in a way that many big cities today would have looked at with serious incredulity. The solution they devised was part-time police.

The phenomenon of part-time police officers is still a common practice in many parts of rural Pennsylvania. It has become such an ingrained practice that its mention hardly raises an eyebrow. Mention such a concept in a large city such as Miami and you would undoubtedly be met with looks of pure disbelief.

Nevertheless, during that era, even among communities that relied on part-time staffing, police service was still a twenty-four-hour-a-day commitment. In order to reduce the costs of full-time benefits such as sick time, vacation time, health insurance and overtime, city leaders would routinely hire only one or two full-time officers and then filled out the remaining staffing needs by hiring as many part-time officers as were necessary.

While these officers were fully sworn police officers, and no less qualified, they were not employed in just one political subdivision. Instead, they split their time among two, three or even four other towns. As a result, the town received the benefit of twenty-four-hour coverage at a bargain-basement cost.

From an officer's point of view, this arrangement created both financial and emotional stress. Many coped by either moonlighting in another line of work or, as most did, by working for many different departments. Even though it did not offer health benefits, insurance or long-term job security, this arrangement did occasionally offer the equivalent of a full-time salary.

It is this odd world into which Leonard Miller was indoctrinated in 1977. In fact, at the time Leonard Miller became a full-time officer, there were only thirty-two full-time officers in all of Armstrong County. To put that into perspective, you should note that Armstrong County encompassed a total of 664 square miles and, according to the 1980 census, was home to over seventy-seven thousand residents.

Like most of his colleagues, Leonard started out as a part-time officer in several towns. Working part-time for Apollo and neighboring Vandergrift and Oklahoma Boroughs, he often worked more-than-forty-hour weeks. It was a hard life, but it was his dream. Leonard had resigned himself to do what he needed to do until something full-time came along—in early 1980, he got his break.

On January 1, 1980, Mayor William Kerr swore in Leonard Miller as a full-time patrol officer for the Borough of Apollo and assigned him badge #78. No longer would Leonard have to divide his time between various employers, working first one set of city streets and then another. For Leonard, it was a dream come true—the chance to be a cop. When Mayor Kerr finally swore him in as Apollo Borough's first African American police officer, Leonard's lifelong dream of becoming a police officer finally materialized. He had realized what many before him had and what many behind him would—public service is its own reward. He would later learn that it is also a great sacrifice.

From the moment that he donned his uniform, among colleagues and citizens alike, he was highly regarded. As both an officer and a man, Leonard commanded tremendous respect. Everyone in town frequently spoke in glowing terms of his kind-hearted nature and positive spirit, and more than one errant youth had Leonard to thank for offering more than mere law enforcement intervention. He was particularly good with young people, and on many occasions he talked them into compliance without ever having to pull out his citation book. He cared about the town, and he cared about the people he served. Leonard Miller was an individual who simply loved life and loved people.

Whether you speak with William Kerr or former officer Jim Clawson, both will agree that Leonard's easygoing nature and carefree outlook made him a giant of a man in both body and spirit.

A big man, Leonard's imposing presence belied a true gentle spirit within, and while ever ready to back up his fellow officer, he was equally quick with a smile or disarming remark. The consummate low-key individual, it took tremendous effort to get Leonard Miller to the point of anger—a quality that endeared him to both colleagues and those he served. For his gentleness of spirit and strength of character, we must thank his parents.

Evelyn and Frank Miller were most proud of these qualities in their son. Their pride extended beyond his dedication to the community to the knowledge that Leonard Miller was a good man, a caring man and one who, for all the evil in the world, had persevered and risen above the fray to find goodness, kindness and redeeming qualities in almost everyone he encountered.

Leonard was quick with a kind word and long on patience. These are the qualities that all parents hope their children attain. The fact that he had become both what he had always aspired to be and good at heart speaks more to the person Leonard Miller was than any other measure. On January 3, 1980, as he sped across the Apollo Bridge in pursuit of three men of incarnate evil, he was a contented man living his dream.

On January 3, Leonard donned badge #78 for the last time. It was a number that would have significance beyond anything that Leonard could have imagined. It became a number that would one day both honor him and warn others of the great sacrifice that he had made in the service of others. Leonard wore the badge proudly, but he wore it, sadly, for only three short days.

The hollow, almost synchronistic *clip-clop, clip-clop* of four feet walking east on Liberty Avenue echoed down the nearly deserted streets as hookers and hustlers scurried along Eighth Street like sewer rats seeking shelter from the blistering winter wind that drove in from the Allegheny River. The two sinewy men with hands stuffed in their pockets and their collars turned up hurriedly ducked under the Harris Theatre marquee. The twinkling lights of the historic Harris Theatre had often signaled refuge and warmth to the dozens of the city's homeless and strays who ducked into midnight showings of *Debbie Does Dallas* or *Deep Throat* to escape the pummeling cold of the city—but not tonight. Tonight, these two downcast strays skipped the show, turned sharply back out to Liberty and, instead, trudged off toward the wretched Edison Hotel.

JOHN LESKO AND HIS WRETCHED EXISTENCE

Thursday, December 27, 1979

The jagged Allegheny winds smacked John Lesko in his drawn, weathered face and forced him to scrunch his head down into his secondhand leather coat. His taller and thinner companion gently wavered to and fro as he adjusted the lamb's wool collar on his jacket. The stiff north wind buffeted both men around like two tiny skiffs on the river. In retaliation, they dropped their dark, greasy-haired heads even deeper into their coats, shoved their hands deeper into their tattered pockets and pushed forward into the night. Each step moved them closer to the warmth of the old, run-down hotel.

In 1979, Liberty Avenue was the heart of Pittsburgh's red-light district. It was home to prostitutes, drug dealers, pimps, hustlers, homosexuals and various other itinerant perverts of all manner and breed. Historic establishments such as the once stately Casino Theatre, which at one time hosted some of vaudeville's brightest stars, had declined into festering cesspools on the south side of the city's north shore.

Liberty Avenue was once a main artery out of the city and ran from picturesque Point State Park all the way out to the well-manicured neighborhood of Shadyside. In the process, it ran straight through the heart of the city, paralleling the Allegheny River and winding through such historic locations as Bloomfield and the Strip District.

The historic Strip District was once a thriving, one-half-square-mile marketplace and warehouse district, filled to the brim with colorful ethnic grocers and peddlers who used to cram the teaming marketplace with their fresh fruits, produce, fish and poultry. It was a bustling thoroughfare and had played host to the commerce and shipping that came straight from the Allegheny River as it made its journey out into the cornucopia neighborhoods that sprawled around the outskirts of the city. Sadly, by the mid-1970s the ravages of urban decline, migration to the suburbs and economic blight had turned many of the historic buildings and the district's once stately architecture into shabby, run-down flophouses, drug dens and fleabag hotels. One such hotel was the Edison.

Located at 135 Ninth Street, on the corner of Ninth and French, the tattered, brown brick façade of the Edison belies its historic pedigree and illustrious but checkered past. Built in 1916, the Edison began its life as a simple one-story saloon. Then, in 1923, thanks to the Volstead Act and

Prohibition, the Edison adopted, at least according to official government records, a "soft drink"–only beverage list. Local lore, however, suggests that the hard-drinking Irish communities that surrounded the hotel may have flocked to its mahogany bar for something a wee bit stiffer than root beer.

In the early 1930s, under new ownership and just coming off a 1928 renovation that added five stories to its height, the Edison became the home-away-from-home to countless vaudeville performers such as Ella Fitzgerald, Sammy Davis Jr. and Pearl Bailey while they performed at the nearby burlesque houses.

With the eventual demise of burlesque, the Edison fell on hard times. Then, in the 1960s, economic necessity brought about its conversion into a topless bar. As with many adult establishments, the conversion brought with it a less desirable and oftentimes less civilized group of clients. By 1979, it had enjoyed a brisk revival, as it offered a steady stream of no-questions-asked hourly customers a safe refuge to ply their trades or simply escape from the cold.

Such was the state of affairs at the Edison Hotel when John Lesko and Michael Travaglia took up residence amidst the flotsam and jetsam that floated into and out of its seventy tumbledown rooms on a daily—or even hourly—basis. In late 1970, prostitutes, johns, drug dealers, hustlers and John Lesko and Michael Travaglia all floated in and out—nameless, faceless and soulless in a world of economic and moral depression.

Perhaps it was the abuse that time had wrought against the Edison Hotel that had drawn John Lesko and Michael Travaglia to it. Or perhaps John Lesko felt a kinship with the building grounded in his own wretched existence. To describe John Lesko's life as Dickensian would hardly be hyperbole. In fact, the record of abuse inflicted on John and his siblings at the hands of their mother and maternal grandmother would make even the most sadistic of Dickens's villains recoil in disbelief.

Born on November 11, 1958, John was the oldest of six children. His mother, Mary Anne Fedorko, had John at the tender age of sixteen and, unsure of the identity of his biological father, chose the surname of Lesko after her paramour at the time of John's birth. The product of an abusive mother herself, Mary Anne Fedorko had embarked on raising her family in the only way she knew—with violence and hatred.

Shortly after John's birth, Mary Anne gave birth to John's half brother, Michael. Unfortunately, by the time of Michael's birth, his father had also disappeared, leaving John, Michael and Mary Anne Fedorko to fend for themselves. John's younger sister, Matilda, or Tilly as they used to call her, was Mary Anne's daughter with Kermit Miller, with whom Mary Anne had one of many brief relationships. Next in line were Kimberly, Joseph and Alicia—all by different and largely unknown fathers, and all brought into a vicious world of drugs, crime and abuse.

When Mary Anne and her children weren't staying with her mother, Anna Ridge, and Mary Anne's sexually abusive stepfather, James Ridge, she was busy shuffling her kids from one rat-infested apartment to another in an effort to stay one step ahead of landlords, bill collectors and the occasional police warrant. Dragging her children to one rathole after another, she occasionally managed to put down roots for several months, only to either abruptly scurry back to her mother's Munhall home or to another equally filthy tenement, two steps ahead of the landlord.

Throughout this time, living conditions were squalid. Frequently without heat, running water or decent furniture, her children slept either on the wooden floor or on a filthy mattress in the corner of the room. When the youngest child, Alicia, was born, an old wooden crate served as her crib for months. When Fedorko finally secured a crib for the infant, a surprised child services worker discovered that the crib was filthy and covered in human feces. This was not the first such visit by child services; nor would it be the last. In fact, child services has memorialized John's entire childhood in volumes of protective services records that could be aptly titled *The Fedorko Family History: Crime and Punishment.*

Frequently disturbed by what they had observed in the various Fedorko homes, child services workers maintained a seven-year-long relationship with the family; however, it was not until matters became unavoidably deplorable that they intervened in any significant way. To say that the health and welfare agencies in Allegheny County had completely failed the Lesko children would be a great understatement.

Underfed, malnourished and clothed only in rags—even in the dead of the frigid Pennsylvania winters—Mary Anne's children were frequently the subject of neglect reports by their various school principals. In hindsight, more than ample grounds existed on numerous occasions for child welfare agencies to remove the children from the home, but John and his brothers and sisters continued to endure a life of filth and squalor. Whether through malfeasance or a desire to keep the family together, child services allowed the children of Mary Anne Fedorko to remain in her care well into John's early teens, even though conditions over the years remained largely unchanged.

Mary Anne Fedorko constantly left the children, some of whom were barely older than infants, home alone. When they weren't running from the rats, they would attempt to heat the apartment with the open flame from the burner on the stove. Additionally, they were forced to do their own laundry in a broken-down ringer washing machine, and they often crushed their fingers trying to manipulate the decrepit apparatus in the freezing, damp basement of their hovel.

When Mary Anne Fedorko *did* come home, it was usually with a steady parade of men—the drunks she would rob, the johns she would charge. Either way, Mary Anne's answer to supplementing her welfare income was always carried out in full view of her six children. In fact, as they got older, Mary Anne enlisted her children's help in going through her paramours' pockets for money as they lay passed out on the flea-infested sofa.

As a disciplinarian, Fedorko was barbaric, unpredictable and ruthless. Prone to wild mood swings, she would fly into a rage at the children and inflict barbaric punishments far out of proportion to whatever perceived misconduct she accused them of. On numerous occasions, she forced the children to kneel on a hot radiator for hours at a time. With their knees burned and bruised, she denied them bathroom privileges. When they eventually wet their pants because they could no longer hold it, Fedorko would beat them with whatever she could get her hands on: a cat-o'-nine-tails, an extension cord or a skillet or frying pan.

Unfortunately for John, as the oldest, he often bore the brunt of his mother's tirades and abuse. Through either intention or circumstance, he seemed to be a magnet for her sharp tongue and quick backhand. Telling him that he was worthless and would amount to nothing, Fedorko constantly reminded John that she "wished he had never been born."

Finally, when John was eleven years old, child services workers intervened. The catalyst was when workers reported that the most recent Fedorko residence was once again rat infested and covered in human and animal feces to the point that their feet actually stuck to the floor. Children's services placed the three oldest children in Holy Family Institute—a group living facility—and Alicia, Kimberly and Joey were placed in foster homes.

During the children's stay at Holy Family, Mary Anne and her mother visited on weekends. Occasionally the children were allowed home visits to their mother's filthy residence, usually on alternate weekends. It was during one of these weekend visits that Mary Anne's boyfriend-of-the-month, Ray Pryzbilinkski, allegedly molested Tilly in the basement. Fearing the repercussions, Mary Anne and Ray blamed John for the abuse, shielding Ray from serious trouble.

As a result, caseworkers separated John and Michael from Tilly and terminated the home visits to the Fedorko residence. Viewed as a more stable environment, visits to the children's grandmother's home were still permitted. Eventually, child welfare authorities gave Anna Ridge full custody of the children. Unfortunately, Anna Ridge was equally abusive.

During John and his siblings' time at Anna Ridge's home, drugs and alcohol became a way of life. From their early years, John and his brother and sister drank, smoked and used drugs. Between exposure to Mary Anne's sisters Joanne and Bunny, who were polydrug addicts and alcoholics, and infrequent supervision, it is little wonder that John and his brothers and sisters turned to drug use. On one occasion, John found his Aunt Joanne's hidden stash of rum. Ever the enterprising youth, he drank the rum and secretly refilled the empty bottles with water.

In John's world, a life of crime was not only accepted, but it was also, in fact, expected. In a scene that could have easily been lifted from a Dickens novel, John's grandmother and aunt turned the children out at night to a life of crime. In the winter, she put the children out on the street with orders not to return to the house without something to show for their efforts. If they did return empty-handed, she locked them out of the house. Even during the bitter cold Pittsburgh winters, Anna Ridge often forced her grandchildren to sleep outside. Occasionally, they were lucky enough to find refuge at a benevolent friend or neighbor's home.

Not surprisingly, John did not fit in at school. Both spotty attendance and poor performance plagued him. The frequently nomadic lifestyle to which Mary Fedorko subjected John and his siblings no doubt aggravated matters.

After school, John sought refuge in the structure and discipline of the Marine Corps. While his initial impressions were enthusiastic, and he seemed to respond quite well to the strict discipline of the corps, he eventually went AWOL. After numerous AWOL charges, John was less-than-honorably discharged and unfortunately was forced to return to the crime-infested, drug-ridden lifestyle from which his brief stint in the marines had freed him.

John's time in the marines had changed him. When he returned, he was much more distant, less talkative and much more out of control. He frequently got into fights, sometimes with little or no provocation. He constantly drank, drove recklessly and appeared to have no fear. John's return from the marines brought not only a return to his former degenerate lifestyle, but it also brought him some disturbing news.

Child welfare had removed John's youngest brother, Joey, from the family well before they had successfully taken the other five kids. Because of this,

Joey was placed in a foster care facility separate from the others. Even though his placement may have saved him from some of his mother's worst abuse, his foster parent subjected him to something far worse. While in foster care, one of his foster care guardians repeatedly abused him sexually.

John was violently upset when he found out about this. Beyond the protective nature of an older brother, John's strong reaction was likely rooted in some early childhood memories of his own.

As a small child roaming the streets and projects of Homestead, amid the steel mills and row houses, John and his brother had run a shoeshine business. For extra money, John carried around his shine kit, and he polished shoes for locals. He tried desperately to put food on the table. On one occasion, one of John's shoeshine patrons invited him back to his home with an offer of more money for another pair of shoes. While at this customer's home, the patron sexually molested him.

These are the formative experiences that John endured. Whether this early abuse was enough of a catalyst to tip the precarious scales of his psychic balance is still up for debate; however, over the next few days, something would align the forces of evil within John enough to bring about a metamorphosis of Kafkan proportion.

Perhaps the grand orchestrator of John's evil rampage was his recent acquaintance, Michael Travaglia. Some argue that while older than John by a mere two months, Michael was the more dominant figure, and as a result, John quickly followed Michael's lead wherever it took the pair.

Regardless of whether John followed or, as others claim, led, the two were destined for infamy from the moment they met.

The two met when both men worked at the Allegheny County Airport. Michael was pursuing training as an airplane mechanic, and both men seemed to find a common bond. Sharing a penchant for drugs and alcohol, the union between these two men forged an alliance that would ultimately lead to the death of four innocent people.

This chance meeting at the Allegheny County Airport in West Mifflin, Pennsylvania, would set in motion seven days of pure, vicious evil. Whether it was John's tortured childhood and cycle of abuse that made him the way he was or whether he was pure and simply born evil, it did not matter—there was something about the derelict and malevolent Edison Hotel that felt like home.

It was this fitting home to which Michael and John were en route when a chance encounter with forty-nine-year-old, unemployed security guard Peter Levato would change history.

As the frigid men walked under the cloudless, coal black city sky, John began thinking about where his next meal was going to come from. Broke, hungry and depressingly sober, they needed some cash—and quick. He sidestepped a tiny bit of debris as it flew past him and then stepped down off the curb onto the street.

They were two blocks from the Edison and gaining ground. The pair crossed the street and picked up their pace.

Peter Levato Becomes the First Victim

The hushed pair braced against the stiff east wind. Liberty Avenue ran north and south, parallel to the Allegheny River, and the ancient granite buildings that stood watch on both sides of the avenue had offered at least some shelter from the blistering winds that whipped off the water. Now, heading down Ninth, free of the shadow of the towering gothic stone structures, the walk was more painful. The men surged forward into the cold. They were almost there.

Halfway down the block, the familiar grayish brown stones of the Edison Hotel came into view, and the scattered, impotent light from the few streetlights barely reached the ground long enough for the men to pick their way through the empty bottles and trash. Hunched over, with their freezing fists punched deeper into their jacket pockets, they pushed forward in determined strides. At first, they didn't notice the gold Ford Grenada as it slowed beside them. The window crept slowly down and Peter Levato stuck out his head.

"You guys want to party?"

Neither man reacted. Seemingly ignorant of the offer, both men continued east toward French Street and the hotel. Peter Levato's two-door crept along beside them.

John leaned into Michael and, in hushed tones, said, "Let's have some fun with this queer."

Michael obviously had a better idea. "Keep walking. I've got a plan."

John continued to the corner and made a quick right onto French Street just beyond the beckoning doors of the Edison Hotel. Michael paused for a moment. The Grenada paused beside him. Stepping into the street and in front of the headlights of Peter Levato's car, he quickly circled around to the driver's side. Michael's lean, wiry frame towered over the open window of

Peter's idling Ford. A warm river of heat spilled out of the car and washed over Michael as he studied Peter Levato's face.

Without warning, Michael ripped open the door and crammed the barrel of a .22-caliber revolver against Peter's temple, freezing him in mid-breath.

"Slide over!" Michael barked.

Peter Levato released his grip on the steering wheel and pushed himself into the passenger's seat with a look of disbelief on his face. In one practiced motion, Michael slid behind the wheel and deftly tapped the horn twice.

On cue, John stepped out from the shadows of French Street into the warm light spilling from the doorway of the Edison. His lean, angular face, half in shadow and half bathed in the warm glow of the Edison, had the appearance of weathered granite as he glanced left, then right. Confident that there were no onlookers, he hustled to the waiting getaway car.

Once John had dropped into the seat beside Peter, sandwiching him between the .22 and John's own stout frame, Michael gunned the engine and sped out of the city toward the suburbs. He seemed energized.

Heading west on Penn Avenue, Michael deftly navigated his way through the confusing one-way streets of the city like a veteran taxi driver until the looming green entrance ramp to Route 376 appeared on the horizon. Heading east, he eased onto the four-lane expressway and settled in for a forty-mile drive.

Deserted and spacious at two o'clock in the morning, the Penn-Lincoln Parkway, simply the "Parkway" to locals, was a straight shot out of the city past Mercy Hospital and the decaying steel mills that lined the Monongahela River. Bordering Schenly and Frick Parks, during the hectic rush hours in Pittsburgh, the Parkway was a bumper-to-bumper morass of suburburanites making their daily trek from the quiet neighborhoods into the city. At this hour, the Grenada sped along in solitude. Michael relaxed his grip on the wheel.

Once they were far out of the city, Michael pulled the car over. All three men piled out of the car—two more readily than the third. Holding Peter at gunpoint, Michael popped the trunk and motioned to John, who began rummaging through its contents. Moments later, John emerged from the shadows with a short length of rope. The men hurriedly wrapped the rope around Peter's wrists and cinched it tight.

Michael eyed Peter, and then he rifled through Peter's pockets, removed his wallet and belongings and motioned for John. The two each grabbed their captive and hoisted the struggling man unceremoniously into the trunk. The hollow thud of Peter's body hitting the trunk floor, followed by the resonant thud of the trunk slamming, echoed endlessly, and Michael quickly counted

Peter's money—fifty-nine dollars. With their mission only half finished, both men jumped into the front seat of what used to be Peter Levato's car, and they were once again eastbound into Westmoreland County.

Disoriented and in darkness, fear gripped Peter. The stench of gasoline and Goodyear was overwhelming. His thoughts darted back and forth as he grappled with what had just happened. What *had* just happened?

The Grenada rattled along the winding highway into the rolling hills outside of Pittsburgh. As they sped farther from the city, fear began to fill Peter's head. He methodically made a checklist in his head: abducted at gunpoint, robbed, tied and heading into the country. He knew that nothing good would come of this. His mind seized on the possibility that death was waiting for him at the end of his journey. He flushed the thought from his mind, determined to think of a plan.

As the car whistled through Five Points and past Shieldburg and New Alexandria, the sounds of the highway and the rhythmic thud of the tires rumbling over the expansion joints were the only sounds that Peter heard. He strained to seize an occasional glimpse of the conversation between his captors, but only wisps of their muffled voices faded in and out of his head. Peter knew that he was alone, bumping along into the night.

As the minutes crept by, Peter's thoughts continued to ricochet. First he abandoned hope and then almost immediately he envisioned a well-played scenario in which he could overpower his captors and make good his escape into the brush. Each time, the buzzing in his brain bounced him from one extreme to the other. His thoughts offered him no comfort.

In the middle of nowhere, surrounded by darkness and pine trees, Michael Travaglia expertly guided the speeding car northward on Route 981 toward Loyalhanna. Conversation was sparse between him and John, and what was unspoken was as telling as what was spoken. Michael knew that John knew what had to be done.

Route 981 gently curved to the right, and Michael slowed. Two hundred yards farther on, invisible in the coal black night, Michael knew that

Loyalhanna Dam Road lurked ahead. He slowed the car, jerked the wheel to the left, turning onto a two-lane road, and then accelerated.

The tiny towns and white-sided churches zipped by as he sped into the night. Tiny homesteads, the occasional farm and diminutive one-horse towns appeared and disappeared along the roadway outside his window. The winding stretch of road leading up to the dam's spillway was desolate. The clear northern sky, cloudless and velveteen, hung over the frosted fields that blanketed both sides of the roadway, and Michael aimed the stolen Ford down the middle. Dodging in and out of the thick, coniferous forests surrounding the dam, the winding two-lane road carried Peter Levato closer to the dark waters of the reservoir with each passing mile. Fifty yards farther ahead, an opening emerged where Loyalhanna Dam Road crossed over Loyalhanna Creek. Michael knew they were close.

The fifty-yard-wide bridge sat twenty feet above the swiftly running waters of Loyalhanna Creek, which left the dam and wended its way to meet its larger sister, the Conemaugh River, at Saltsburg.

Skidding to a stop on the southwest side of the bridge, Michael threw the car into park and shut off the ignition. Instantly, the dark, still silence of the steep, wooded hillsides enveloped both men. Even the rushing headwaters of the spillway were distant, faint whispers as they escaped the Loyalhanna Dam and rolled down through the limestone rock and the crispness of the frozen world. In the stillness of the wintry night, the river swallowed up even their thoughts. Michael moved first and stepped out onto the bridge.

The metallic chatter of keys pierced the silence. The sharp *thunk-click* of the trunk lock and then the rusty creak of the Grenada's trunk lid hinge rattled through the leafless trees along the riverbank. It startled a family of opossums that were innocently foraging for grubs under the concrete abutment, and they quickly dove beneath some rocks near the creek's edge.

Michael looked down at Peter Levato's cold, motionless body. It looked stiff from the nearly hour-and-a-half ride out of the city. Peter began to stir. Startled by his sudden movement, Michael raised the revolver over his head and viciously crushed it down onto Peter's skull. Tiny rivulets of blood trickled down Peter's forehead. Shoving the gun into his waistband, Michael motioned to John and then grabbed the dazed Levato and began to hoist him from the trunk.

Both men struggled with opposite ends of Peter Levato's wriggling body. They maneuvered him from the well of the trunk and carried him to the concrete retaining wall that separated them from the icy creek twenty feet below. Unceremoniously, they hurled his bruised and dazed body over the edge. Michael thought to himself how easy it had been as he listened to the splash echo off the valley walls and dissolve into the night. The silence once again overpowered the night air.

Suddenly, a commotion erupted from under the bridge. A cacophonous barrage of splashes and screams echoed from under the concrete piling. Peering over the edge, Michael could see nothing in the darkness. Peter Levato's screams of pure desperation grew louder and more frantic.

Determined not to go quietly into the night, Peter pulled his hands from the ropes and began to swim to shore. Although fewer than one hundred yards wide at the bridge, the ice cold temperatures made an otherwise routine swim across the creek nearly impossible. As he struggled against the cold and swift current of the creek, Peter's flailing alerted John and Michael, who were standing above him staring down into the swirling water beneath the bridge. They didn't react. Maybe they didn't see him, Peter thought.

Moments later, with frantic, irate energy, Michael and John sprinted to the west end of the bridge and scrambled down the embankment. Sliding on the leaf litter and broken branches that had collected over the past autumn, they reached the riverbank in seconds.

The men paused and listened. The sounds of snapping twigs and crunching leaves followed Peter as he reached the shore and raced headlong down the riverbank and into the woods. Peter could hear his pursuers as they carefully picked their way along the thick, tree-lined river's edge after him.

Peter's swim and subsequent flight had left him gasping for breath. Cold, exhausted and disoriented, miles from the nearest building and entirely dependent on himself for salvation, his body commanded that he rest—just for a minute. He slipped behind the largest tree he could find. Carefully, he maneuvered to put the tree between his pursuers and himself, and then he listened. There was no sound. The snapping of twigs and crunching of leaves had stopped.

Crouched against the tree, Peter struggled for breath and willed his heart to slow and his hands to stop shaking. Whether from the cold, fear or exertion, his whole body was quivering uncontrollably. No matter how hard he tried, he could not make it stop.

Peter still didn't hear anything. He saw even less. Squinting his eyes in the velvet black darkness, he searched and searched. He still saw nothing.

A shadow darted in front of him. Instantly, both his pursuers were upon him. Pinned against the tree, Peter's killers had left him nowhere to go. As they towered over his crouching, freezing body, Michael Travaglia gripped the knurled handle of a .22 and aimed for the middle of Peter's body.

The staccato report from the gun startled all three men as tiny orange flames lit up the leafy ground around their feet. When the bullet struck Peter Levato in the chest, it instantly dropped him to his knees. The relentless searing-lead torpedo tore through his chest and into the flailing, faltering muscles of his heart. They seized instantly. He crumpled to the ground in a lifeless mass.

Michael was obviously not satisfied. He walked deliberately and confidently toward Peter Levato's motionless body and quickly fired two more shots. *Bang! Bang!* Both struck Levato's lifeless body in the top of the head and bored down into his now vacant brain.

For all the deafening commotion of the past two minutes, the banks of the Loyalhanna Creek were now eerily silent—deadly silent. Peter Levato was dead. Michael Travaglia and John Lesko had begun their seven-day reign of terror. The kill for thrill had begun.

Part II

Edward Wolak Finds the Body

On Friday, December 28, 1979, an event so innocuous that it would go unnoticed for two days occurred. Yet it was an event so profound that when Sergeant Tom Tridico later heard of it, it would prove to be the first link in a chain of evidence that would lead Michael Travaglia, John Lesko and Tom Tridico into a head-on collision.

Without fanfare and with little more than routine police effort, officers of the Penn Township Police Department had stumbled on the stubbly stalks of a quiescent cornfield in a remote part of the outskirts of Delmont, Pennsylvania. Located behind Joe's Steakhouse on Route 22 near the interchange for Pennsylvania's Turnpike, the snow-draped field had rested in undisturbed winter slumber until, shortly after executing Peter Levato, Michael Travaglia and John Lesko dumped his 1975 gold Ford Grenada among the field's spent husks.

When the Penn Township Police discovered Peter's car abandoned and unoccupied, officers did what any member of a respectable municipal police department would do with an abandoned vehicle—they checked the license plate to see if it had been reported stolen. It had not. Without a crime to investigate, the police followed the next step in the procedure for dealing with abandoned vehicles—they towed it to an impoundment facility.

For Sergeant Tom Tridico, the discovery of Peter Levato's Grenada by the Penn Township Police would normally be nothing more than a tiny bump in the workday life of an investigative supervisor for the Pennsylvania State Police. In fact, chances are, had it not been for the events of the next few days, Tom Tridico might have finished the remainder of this thirty-three years with the state police having never even heard Peter Levato's name.

Tom Tridico grew up in Warren, Pennsylvania, a small town about forty minutes southeast of Erie and about five minutes from the New York–Pennsylvania state line. Tom's father was the fire chief in Warren, and from an early age, he was attracted to police work. Growing up near the state police barracks in Erie helped, and shortly after ending his three-year naval enlistment, Tom signed up for the Pennsylvania State Police.

In 1947, he graduated from the State Police Academy in Hershey, Pennsylvania. He had finally realized his dream. He was a cop. Tom was assigned the rank of private. Over the course of his career, Tom Tridico would serve in a number of capacities; however, the one for which he would become most well known was his position as the supervisor of criminal investigations for the Troop A barracks of the Pennsylvania State Police in Greensburg, Pennsylvania.

In this capacity, Tom oversaw the criminal investigation of his troop. He reviewed their cases, assigned them to investigations and, when cases like the Travaglia and Lesko one arose, he would coordinate the investigation. Supervising men such as Charles Lutz, Richard Dickey, Curtis Hahn, Robert Luniewski and countless others, Tom Tridico would eventually call upon them to bring Michael Travaglia and John Lesko to justice.

By Tridico's own count, he has handled thousands of criminal investigations and well over two hundred homicide investigations. Nevertheless, the Travaglia and Lesko case has most affected him. Probably in part because of Leonard Miller and in part because, as the years have dragged on, the criminal justice system has called on him to repeatedly recount for jurors and jurists alike the soul-robbing events that began for him on the cusp of the New Year in 1980. In 1979, Tom Tridico did not know Edward Wolak. Tom Tridico did not know Peter Levato. Soon, however, Edward Wolak would know both Peter Levato and Tom Tridico.

Snow crunched beneath Edward Wolak's boots as he picked his way down the bank into the ravine below. It was getting late in the morning. He ducked beneath the snow-draped branch of a spruce tree. "Just one more trap to check," he mumbled, "and then home in time for lunch."

The feeble morning sun peeked through the trees behind him as he made his way along the steep bank, squashing the dappled sunlight with his hunting boots. One hundred feet beyond, a fallen oak tree stretched across the mouth of the ditch. The long-retired patriarch of the glen marked the spot where Eddie's next trap lay in wait, with its famished mouth open wide, eagerly awaiting its next meal. He squeezed under the recumbent oak and knelt beside the trap. It was empty. It was always empty. He didn't expect today to be much different than any other day. The only things two years of trapping in these woods had earned him were a few mangy squirrels, an opossum and one rather scruffy beaver pelt.

He stood up, brushed the forest litter from the knees of his brown corduroy pants and shuffled his thick rubber boots through the ankle-deep layer of leafy debris. As he followed the gently curving ditch toward a large stand of evergreens, the rush of the creek behind him drowned out his thoughts.

The chains of the two galvanized steel-jawed traps that hung over his left shoulder rhythmically jangled and clanked in his ear to the beat of his rising and falling feet. He adjusted them with a gloved hand and pushed through a wall of pine boughs like a passenger forcing his way onto the subway.

By now, the sun had climbed into the late morning cerulean sky, and as he stepped onto the road, the muted world of the ravine receded into his memory. He looked up. Tears filled his squinting eyes as they struggled to adjust to the solar onslaught. Eddie lifted his hand to shield his eyes and stared down the road leading back toward his house, where he knew a warm lunch would surely greet him. As he crossed Loyalhanna Dam Road and headed for the banks of Loyalhanna Creek, he hoped that his Saturday morning had not been a total waste.

Eddie scattered some loose twigs with the toes of his boots as he walked. Silent thoughts of lunch wrapped around him like a warm blanket as step after step rose and fell, bringing him closer and closer to his home. As he picked his way through the underbrush, his eyes were drawn to the base of a large tree sitting about twenty feet from the edge of the creek. He moved in for a closer look.

Growing out of the side of the tree was what looked like an odd, twisted branch. It was misshapen and knurled. As Edward circled the tree, a sharp bit of sunlight caught his eye and everything flashed white. He rubbed his eye with wool-gloved fists and took two more steps. Standing in the long shadow of the large tree, Edward Wolak slowly reopened his eyes.

He was staring into Peter Levato's lifeless face. An invisible fist landed squarely in Eddie's gut with a dull thud. It forced every thread of air out of his lungs, while microscopic tremors crept into his boots. They inched up his legs, knocking his knees together like bowling pins until his quivering hands dangling by his sides shivered in chaotic gyration. The two vacant eyes fixed on him through puffy, blood-smeared cheeks. He could not move; he could not even breathe.

Trooper Charles Lutz was the investigator with Troop A who received the call from Ed Wolak on that late December afternoon. As luck or misfortune would have it, he was the duty investigator assigned for that weekend, and fate had put him in the right place at the right time. The desolate, post-Christmas barracks was silent. Empty except for a few critical employees, the barracks gave Chuck Lutz time to be alone with his thoughts.

Most of the troopers assigned to patrol were already out blanketing their assigned areas, and the sporadic crime that occasionally stirred in the valley was obviously on Christmas hiatus, so Chuck relaxed at his desk. As he did, he thumbed through stale cases and drank stale coffee.

At 12:30 p.m., the clattering ring of the phone snapped Chuck back into 1979. He lifted the receiver from its cradle and the voice of his boss, Sergeant Tom Tridico, began to rattle off names and locations. Scribbling in his own brand of shorthand onto his desk blotter, he grunted and "Yupped" his way through the next three minutes of the morning. A reassuring, "I'm on it," ended the official call, and Charles Lutz lowered the black Bakelite receiver onto its resting place.

He scooped up his jacket from the back of the chair and quickly poked two arms through the sleeves. Then he gathered his notebook from his desk, tucked it into his inside jacket pocket and slid open his desk drawer. Slipping the stainless steel Ruger .357 revolver into its holster, he slammed the drawer shut, adjusted his jacket over his holster and grabbed the keys to his police interceptor. He quickly slipped out of the squad room and headed down the stairs and out the back door of the barracks. Chuck Lutz did not know that waiting for him below the Loyalhanna Dam was a murder investigation that would last for thirty years.

He headed out Route 66 from the barracks, mentally preparing for a routine death investigation. With the afternoon sun at his back, he quickly sped along the hilly highway, turned onto 380 and then slipped down into the winding valleys leading out to Loyalhanna Reservoir. Each mile drew him closer and closer to Peter Levato. He turned sharply onto Loyalhanna Dam Road and headed down toward the bridge.

Meet Michael Travaglia

Michael Travaglia was a nice kid. By many accounts, this unassuming, nondescript youth was virtually indistinguishable from every other student at Kiski Area Senior High. Snuggled into the rolling pastures forty miles east of Pittsburgh, Kiski was a brand-new school when Michael began there in 1973.

A thin youth, Michael was tall for his age and quite shy. The younger of two children, Michael was born on August 31, 1958, to Bernard and Judith Travaglia. Bernard, his father, was a strict disciplinarian with a low tolerance for poor behavior. His disciplinary tactics went beyond normal definitions of authoritarian rule—even, perhaps, bordering on abusive.

Michael's mother's affection toward her youngest son bordered on cold and distant. She was an extremely religious woman and not one who was ready to show her two boys tremendous warmth and affection. Later in life, her failing health would take her before her time, leaving Bernard alone to face the drawn-out appeals waged by his son. In the end, both of Michael's parents would distance themselves from their youngest son, neither visiting nor corresponding while their son sat on death row.

For whatever faults Michael's father may have had, he was not lazy. He was, in fact, a very hard worker. A plasterer in business with his brother, Bernard Travaglia worked hard to provide his wife and two children with a well-kept home among the greening hills of Washington Township outside Apollo.

Bernard and his wife lovingly tended the Travaglia homestead as it perched atop a hill in tiny Paulton. Trying to make it a safe and inviting home for their two boys, they both worked hard and long hours. From the well-manicured lawn to the garage and shop in the back, it was a picturesque testament to rural life.

While some sibling rivalry is typical in all families, the dissention that existed between Michael and his brother, Kenneth, was beyond what most would consider normal. Preceding him in school by a year, Michael always saw Kenneth as the favored son, and whether real or perceived, this partiality by Michael's parents toward his older sibling created great pressures for him.

As a student, many of Michael's teachers spoke fondly of him. Some even testified as character witnesses on his behalf during his trial. Whether it was his swimming coach or Michael Lamendola, his symphonic band instructor, they described him as well behaved, straight-laced and incapable of committing such heinous atrocities as the news accounts had attributed to him.

A neighbor to the Travaglia family once described him as a timid boy who, when visiting their home to play with their son, wouldn't even come into the kitchen without permission.

Other neighbors described a far different boy. This Michael Travaglia tortured small animals and displayed a disturbing mean streak.

His school record at Kiski Area Senior High School was, like most of Michael's early years, unremarkable. He graduated in 1976 and shortly thereafter began training as an airplane mechanic. Studying at the Allegheny County Airport near Mount Pleasant, just outside Pittsburgh, Michael had a knack for the mechanical. Doing well in school, his training moved along as planned until late 1979. It was then that Michael first met John Lesko.

In hindsight, one might be tempted to speculate on the effect that the ultra-strict upbringing of Bernard and Judith Travaglia had on Michael. Whether his escape from the heavy-handedness of his father might have lent a strong push toward his eventual collapse into total chaos is unknown. Many have made such speculation, yet none has hit upon the definitive answer. Perhaps, as with a great deal of human behavior issues, no singular answer exists.

Whether attributable to a newfound freedom or his newly formed friendship with John Lesko—with its concomitant orgiastic feast of drugs and alcohol—something changed in Michael Travaglia after his graduation.

Although more than fifty witnesses testified to Michael's good character, many of Michael's post-incarceration writings hint at a very different child—a child prone to drug and alcohol abuse at an early age.

A self-professed Satanist at the time of his arrest, Michael claims that incarceration, as it does for many, has changed him. One such change has been a turn toward Christianity.

As with any claim of prison conversion, strong skepticism is warranted. While his current religious beliefs are 180 degrees from what he claimed in

1979, whether this is genuine or artificial, society will never know. The blank stare of impending death often changes a person's outlook.

In addition to, or perhaps because of, his miraculous turn toward God, Michael has married a woman he met in prison. He originally met his wife, Fran Andrasy, through her church, and she first visited him on Christmas Day 1990. Two years later, in a "contact" prison ceremony, Fran Andrasy became Fran Travaglia. Even though the couple has been married fifteen years, their union is anything but conventional.

As a death row inmate, Travaglia is not allowed contact visits. Therefore, visitation between Mr. and Mrs. Travaglia is limited to Bible study sessions conducted from opposite sides of bulletproof glass. Seated across from Michael, separated by two inches of Plexiglas, Fran reads passages from the Bible that she and her husband selected earlier. Sharing in this communion of spirit brings Fran Travaglia some peace of mind. The rest of the community is not quite so reassured.

Attesting to his wholesale change in personality, Fran Travaglia is quick to speak in her husband's defense. She urges all who will listen to consider the possibility that the Michael Travaglia from 1979 is not the same Michael Travaglia of 2008. In addition to these outward manifestations of change, Michael has undertaken some rather extensive writing.

Michael's Internet writings proclaim his newfound Christian faith and offer a contrite outlook. They also offer a tiny glimpse into what may have played a part in his demonic snap in 1979.

In one such writing, Michael claims to have begun a pattern of drug and alcohol abuse during his high school years. He confesses that he began with beer, graduated to whiskey and vodka and moved on to all kinds of drugs, including marijuana and mescaline, and eventually developed an addiction to amphetamines. Surely, this drug- and alcohol-abusing Satanist is a far step from what character witnesses described as a good man, incapable of committing four murders.

Regardless of the identity of the catalyst that precipitated his fall, Michael's spiral downward was rapid, violent and beyond question. We will debate the whys and the hows of Michael's demise for the rest of time. What is certain, though, is that in the wee hours of Monday, December 30, 1979, Michael Travaglia, in the company of his partner John Lesko, found himself on Route 22 in Delmont without a car, without money and looking for more thrills.

Scattering rocks with their shuffling feet, Michael and John picked their way west along Route 22. The shoulder of the highway was stony and sloped quickly away from the edge of the highway. Walking was difficult, but having abandoned their only transportation the night before, the pair was forced to trudge along on foot.

Michael and John were headed to a room that they had rented at Thatcher's Motel. It was a stone's throw from the stubbly cornfield behind Joe's Steakhouse where they had dumped Peter Levato's car. The short half-mile walk on William Penn Highway to the motel seemed endless in the subzero blistering winds. They complained silently to themselves as warm, happy motorists zipped out of and back into the darkness.

Around the bend, the single-story mom and pop motel in the old motor lodge style sat beckoning them. It was small—tiny actually. It had barely a dozen rooms for rent. In fact, if not for the towering red and white roadside sign advertising "ROOMS," the motel would barely be noticeable from the roadway. Hidden neatly behind several full-grown spruce trees, its rustic, A-frame roof and tidy, white wooden pillars were an unopened invitation to weary guests to shake the road dust off and "stay a spell."

Finally, having arrived at their destination, Michael slipped the key into the door lock and walked inside. They had returned to their room. They were hungry, broke and unsure of their next move, but for now, they were warm.

Inside the cramped motel room, dozens of empty beer cans rattled around. Every step the men took risked disturbing a bit of trash or discarded can. Colorful flowered bedspreads had been balled up and carelessly flung across the room, where they landed in a heap near the corner. Half-filled beer bottles, cigarette stubs and fast-food wrappers sat piled up on the pale yellow lowboy that cowered beneath the hanging mirror on the west wall of the tiny room.

Rifling through the rubbish, Michael scoured the place for food, beer, grass—anything. Everywhere he looked, he found nothing. His stomach was no longer satisfied with the few scraps of food since his last full meal—compliments of Peter Levato's fifty-nine dollars—and his head chimed in. Swollen and throbbing, it screamed ceaseless orders with an unrelenting vigor. He needed to shut them up.

With the rent overdue and no money left in their pockets, creative thinking was required if they expected to stay warm, fed and high for very long. Armed robbery had gotten them this far. Yesterday they had added murder to their credit, and Michael was determined that somehow they would put some food in their bellies. Fortunately, Michael didn't limit his creativity to legal alternatives. Once again, he knew exactly what to do.

With renewed resolve fueled by his growing hunger and fading intoxication, Michael gathered a few of life's essentials and stuffed them into a bag. Within minutes, he and John stepped back out onto the bleached concrete porch of the quaint motel. Michael pulled the door closed behind them, and they set off into the frigid night to find their next exploit.

While Michael and John set out into the cold, the man who would ultimately bring them to justice lay fast asleep in the warmth of his Greensburg home. Tom Tridico was dreaming of eventual retirement and a life away from men like Michael Travaglia and John Lesko.

Homicide investigators bump up against the worst that society has to offer. Not only must they confront the horrors of a life snuffed out in violence and anger, but they must also meet head on the pain heaped upon those left behind.

Training and experience can guard against the revulsion you feel when you walk into a crime scene littered with gray matter, human flesh, blood and half-putrefied remains. The deeper, more lasting emotional scars that often plague experienced homicide investigators are hazards that no amount of training can help you avoid.

Meeting the challenge of comforting those for whom a loved-one's demise is both untimely and exceedingly violent forces the homicide investigator to walk a precariously thin line between compassion and dispassion. On the one hand, compassion for the victim, his family and loved ones allows the investigator to do what his training tells him to do—speak for those who cannot speak. On the other hand, compassion, empathy and identification with the survivors can lead to over involvement and tremendous emotional burdens.

If they wish to survive, homicide investigators learn early on that the things they do cannot become personal. Personal involvement, when it occurs, will bring with it the inevitable feelings of loss, emotional struggle and failure when the inevitable happens—and it always does.

Even though statistics show that of all major crimes, homicides are usually the most solvable, there will be times when even the most dedicated efforts fail to deliver anyone in handcuffs. When this happens, overly impassioned investigators risk falling prey to their own self-doubts and feelings of failure—feelings that, if left unchecked, can lead to further psychological issues such as alcoholism, depression and even suicide.

Veteran homicide investigators develop a tough, callous exterior—a shell—something to protect them from witnessing, day-in and day-out, things unimagined by the average person. The depth of man's depravity and the violence of which he is capable is branded into the homicide investigator's psyche at nearly every crime scene. Whether it is husband against wife, child against parent or stranger against stranger, there is a never-ending parade of horrific and unspeakable acts that confront a homicide investigator over the course of his career.

For the average citizen, these seamy incidents are the stuff of movies, tabloids and the six o'clock news. For the homicide investigator, they are a way of life—a way of life that cannot be ignored.

Tom Tridico was such an investigator. Surviving thirty years in the trenches is a testament to the skill with which he had navigated these turbulent seas. Avoiding such common "cop" pitfalls as alcoholism, divorce and suicide, Tom had weathered the storm. He had persevered. That is, until now.

History was yet to write the final chapters of Tom Tridico's celebrated career. At 5:00 a.m. on Sunday, December 30, 1979, the game was afoot. Events had been set in motion from which the story of his life would emerge. As he dozed peacefully in the warmth of his two-story house in the sleepy county seat of Westmoreland County, Tom Tridico's dreams could not prepare him for what he was about to encounter. In fewer than ten days, history would link the names of Michael Travaglia and John Lesko indelibly and irrevocably with Sergeant Tom Tridico.

At 9:00 a.m., Rich Dickey and George Boyerinas each hovered over his desk, coffee in hand. They were killing time at the Kiski Valley Barracks, waiting for Tom Tridico and his regularly scheduled intelligence meeting. Sharing information among investigators was a big deal to Tridico—it helped spot patterns. It helped solve cases. Peter Levato's frozen corpse was on the agenda for this morning. He was John Doe #1.

When Tridico arrived at the barracks, he gathered his investigators around and began talking, listening and thinking. He told of a hunter named Ed Wolak and how the crime scene was straightforward. John Doe's killer had bound him with common white cotton rope, but he had somehow managed to free himself. The condition of the body hinted that he had been in the water but had managed to swim to shore and climb out onto the bank. His pockets were empty, and there were signs that his killer had beaten him.

The autopsy revealed that the suspect shot him three times with a .22-caliber weapon at close range. The first shot entered his chest and pierced his heart, and then the killer fired the next two shots at close range into the back of his skull. The crime scene technicians scoured the surrounding woods but found no identification, money or personal effects near the body. As odd as it sounded, Tridico noted that the suspect had removed Peter Levato's dentures. These were the insipid little details of Peter Levato's death, and he relayed them in all their clinical sterility.

After fielding a few questions about John Doe, Tridico steered the meeting toward the rest of the day's business. A rash of robberies was troubling the Indiana barracks, the local police had handled a few local burglaries and overall, with the exception of John Doe, it was shaping up to be a very calm Christmas season.

As Tom Tridico wrapped up his meeting, he scanned the teletype printouts from the past several days. His eyes drifted down the page. A litany of "Be on the look-outs," all-points bulletins and missing endangered persons announcements were scattered among the names of wanted felons and escaped prisoners sent out across the state. One entry caught his eye. The Penn Township Police had recovered an abandoned 1975 Ford Grenada in a field along Route 22 near Joe's Steakhouse.

Tridico pulled the printout off the stack. The registration of the vehicle listed forty-nine-year-old Peter Levato of 3120 Mount Hope Road in Pittsburgh as the owner. Sensing that these seemingly unrelated pieces of information might be tied together, Tridico sent Trooper Curtis Hahn and Detective George Boyerinas to canvass Peter Levato's Mount Hope neighborhood. He sent a photograph of Chuck Lutz's John Doe with them just in case.

THE CASE OF THE STOLEN KIELBASA

It wasn't long after Hahn and Boyerinas began showing the photograph around that neighbors positively identified the man as Peter Levato. Peter

Levato was now the first official victim of Michael Travaglia and John Lesko. He now had the dubious distinction of being the tip of a four-murder iceberg that would emerge from the frozen waters surrounding the Alle-Kiski Valley.

Unfortunately, as with most criminal investigations, the information on the murder of Peter Levato came in fits and spurts. To the lament of Tom Tridico, the search of both Peter Levato's 1975 Grenada and the cornfield behind Joe's Steakhouse revealed very little new information about his killers. Because of either extreme care or pure accident, John Lesko and Michael Travaglia had left behind few tangible clues.

The true irony of the search of the Joe's Steakhouse cornfield lies in the fact that, as Sergeant Tom Tridico and Rich Dickey combed the frozen earth of the field in search of a link to Peter Levato's killer, Michael Travaglia and John Lesko lay passed out in the warmth of their rented beds at Thatcher's Motel. Slumbering in their drug-clouded, dreamless sleep, Peter Levato's killers were less than one mile from the police dragnet. The first meeting between police and the murderous duo was not to be on that brisk December day. For that, Tridico would have to wait four more days.

As the first real day of progress in the Peter Levato murder investigation ended, members of Pennsylvania State Police's Kiski Valley Barracks were on the cusp of a discovery for which they were not prepared. Tom Tridico in particular left his office at the end of his tour comfortably knowing that he and his men were working a random, or at least uncomplicated, murder. The facts that had emerged suggested to these trained investigators that Peter Levato had been killed as part of a robbery.

In homicide parlance, detectives call it presentation—the body position, scene condition and circumstances of the scene. In Peter Levato's case, everything pointed to a robbery and murder; a scenario that, between them, they had seen dozens of times. Nonetheless, Peter Levato's frozen corpse, now disemboweled, embalmed and en route to his final earthen rest, had brought forth key clues that would eventually resonate throughout the barracks like a thunderclap.

It is fitting that the final day of the decade that was the '70s would bring forth the important clues that would eventually signal the final days of Michael Travaglia and John Lesko's rampage. Although New Year's Eve

1979 began no different from the 363 days that had preceded it, it would end quite differently, for Michael and John and for the men who were doggedly pursuing them.

Early on this last Monday in December, Sergeant Tridico assembled his men again—among them Trooper Rich Dickey and George Boyerinas—and conducted his standard briefing and status review.

In a homicide investigation, valuable clues to the identity of the killer often come from what detectives refer to as the victimology—the tiny minutiae that make up who we are. Victimology includes such mundane details as where we shop, with whom we associate and what sort of lifestyle we lead. The answer to questions such as "Do we engage in drug use?" or "Are we a church deacon?" will point to two very different lifestyles. These lifestyle clues can lead to many theories about what led to our death.

Gathering information about who Peter Levato was topped Tom Tridico's list of things to accomplish before the New Year dawned. In pursuit of this vital information, Tridico assigned Dickey and Boyerinas the rather boring job of conducting a background check. While Hahn and Boyerinas's original neighborhood canvass had revealed what little neighbors actually knew about the man at 3120 Mount Hope Road, they needed many more details if they hoped to crack this case—details such as his employment record.

Peter used to work for Universal Security as a guard. According to the chief of the Bigelow Apartments Security force, he had worked for them up until the early part of December. After Universal fired Peter, the Cauley Detective Agency on Penn Avenue hired him, sometime around December 14, but had not scheduled him to report for his first shift until Friday, December 28, at 8:00 p.m. He never showed up for work. No one from Cauley had heard from Peter Levato since.

Peter had few close acquaintances, and those whom investigators did find began to paint a picture of a man who led a life of relative solitude. He was briefly married to Mary Levato. They had no children, and they had been separated for some time on the day he disappeared. She hadn't heard from him either.

Peter Levato had a criminal record. In 1950, Pittsburgh police had arrested Peter for the offense of public indecency. Then, in 1973, a judge placed him on two years of probation after another arrest. This time, Pittsburgh police had arrested Peter for indecent sexual assault. In isolation, these arrests were not particularly telling; however, when coupled with the snippets of his personal life detectives had collected from friends and family, they began to allow detectives to see a clearer picture of Peter Levato.

Police now believed that Peter Levato might have been gay. If that were the case, then something in his lifestyle might have triggered his abduction. Tridico and his men began to explore the possibility that his killer may have abducted and robbed him because of his sexual orientation.

Monday, December 31, 1979

In the world of criminal investigations, there are glamorous cases and there are dreary cases—the sexy, glamorous cases that make the top half of the evening news and the dreary cases that rarely even make the inside pages of the daily paper. The truth is that 80 percent of police work consists of mundane, dreary cases. The other 20 percent, however, can lead a detective to rapid advancements.

The bread-and-butter, dreary, everyday cases often result in mind-numbing monotony. They perpetuate a "what's the sense of it all" outlook. Chuck Lutz resigned himself to the fact that the call he was about to answer was definitely among the lot of the dreary and far from the spotlight often hovering around the sexy. Chuck Lutz caught the case of the stolen kielbasa.

The call arrived at about 10:30 a.m., and it was again Chuck Lutz's misfortune to be in the wrong place at the wrong time. Dispatchers sent him out to Sonny's Lounge on Route 22 to handle a delayed burglary. Shortly after his arrival, he met with the owner. The hyperactive owner handed Chuck a list of the booty that unknown thieves had stolen from his bar. Rattling off details that Chuck really didn't need to know, this Sherlock Holmes in training speculated that the burglary occurred sometime between 4:00 a.m. yesterday (Sunday) morning and just before 10:00 a.m. this morning—when he called the police.

With all the professionalism and courtesy that makes the Pennsylvania State Police one of the premiere law enforcement organizations in the nation, Chuck Lutz judiciously recorded the haul in his notebook:

$150 in change from the cigarette machine
1 bottle of Jack Daniel's whiskey
1 bottle of Canadian Club whiskey
1 bottle of gin
A six-pack of Stroh's beer
A little more than a case of Miller beer

A five-pound package of Land O'Lakes cheese
A one-and-a-half-pound container of Luger kielbasa

Having painstakingly noted, in exact detail, the extensive list of missing items whose grand total was all of a couple hundred dollars, Chuck continued his investigation by walking around the building.

The back window was ajar. It was probably the point of entry. Chuck threw some fingerprint powder around the area and then snapped a few photographs. After fifteen or twenty minutes without much solid evidence, Chuck decided to wrap it up. He walked out of the drafty little bar onto the bleached concrete sidewalk and headed to the next-door business to begin his canvass.

The shade of the towering pine trees covered the concrete walkway making the already frozen air practically arctic. He covered the distance in long, even strides. One final step and he was staring the rustic white door in the face. Wrapping his gloved hand around the knob, he gave it a twist and flung the door open. The warmth wrapped around him the moment he ducked his six-foot frame into the tiny lobby of Thatcher's Motel.

From behind the counter, a diminutive, balding man stared up into the trooper's face with a look that meant that he knew this must be an official visit.

"I'm investigating a burglary next door at Sonny's Lounge. It happened sometime between Sunday morning and 10:30 this morning…Did you see or hearing anything?"

"Really? No, I didn't notice anything." He paused. "What'd they take? Anything much?"

Chuck Lutz slipped off his calfskin gloves and laid them on the counter. As he lifted the spiral notebook from his inside breast pocket, he said, "Nothing of much value, probably just some kids." As the top flap of the notebook flopped open, he continued, "Some food. Kielbasa…cheese…lots of liquor…and 'bout 150 bucks in change from the cigarette machine."

With a flick of his wrist, he closed the notebook and slid it behind the flap of his jacket. As he scooped up his gloves and turned toward the door in an attempt to get back to some real police work, the manager spoke up. "You know, I didn't hear nothing." He paused. "But there were these two guys in room twelve."

Lutz shifted his weight back toward the counter.

"I evicted 'em yesterday. I think they had a bunch of coins on a towel in the room when I went in, as I recall. I kicked 'em out for not paying for the room. It was a mess, too."

Perhaps this case would be a clearance after all, Lutz thought. "Do you know their names?"

The manager hoisted a dog-eared register from the counter and flipped it open to a paper-clipped page. As he ran his finger down the sparse list of names, he paused. "Michael Travaglia. I don't know the other guy but I think his name might be Daniel something." He paused again. "Keith. Daniel Keith, I think maybe that's his name. That was part of the reason I kicked 'em out. Only supposed to be one person in the room you know... That and the money he owed me."

Retrieving his notebook, Lutz began copying the register information.

"This guy's been in here before, too, with another guy. He uses the name Michael Simmons sometimes," the manager added.

When Chuck Lutz was done writing, he looked up from his notebook and asked, "May I see the room?"

"Sure." The innkeeper grabbed a green, diamond-shaped key off the pegboard and then waddled around the counter toward the door. "I kicked them out yesterday about four in the afternoon. I haven't had the chance to clean the place yet." He paused, scanning the empty motel parking lot. "Not that I guess it matters," he quipped.

Cautiously peering through the tiny window flanked by perfect tiny white shutters, Lutz reassured himself that the room was, in fact, vacant. Moments later, the manager was bounding into the room and shaking his head. "See. A mess. What a bunch of pigs."

Lutz scanned the room. A half dozen empty Stroh's beer cans were scattered around the room with empty Land O'Lakes cheese wrappers and other assorted trash. Lying in the bottom of the trash can, Lutz noticed a large, gelatinous brick of half eaten Land O'Lakes cheese. Satisfied that the perpetrators of the Sonny's caper were the former occupants of room twelve, Chuck Lutz nodded his thanks to the manager and turned to head out the door.

Doggedly following him, the manager spoke, "You know, they left some belongings with me. Told me they'd be back last night by eleven with the rent money to pick 'em up. They never came." He shook his head in disappointment.

Once again inside the warmth of the tiny motel lobby, Chuck Lutz hovered over two large garbage bags perched atop the registration counter. Pawing through them, he withdrew a few items of interest. Mixed among some assorted clothing and personal belongings were a bottle of Jack Daniel's whiskey, a bottle of VO gin, some Luger kielbasa and a stack of papers.

Rummaging through the papers, he stopped at the stack of mail. Lutz began recording the details—Michael Travaglia, RD 4, Apollo.

One particular item caught his attention. It was a letter addressed to Michael Travaglia from the Leechburg Bank notifying him that they were repossessing his 1979 GMC pickup truck. He gathered up several of the pieces of mail and tucked them into a bag, and then, satisfied that he had as much information as he needed, Trooper Chuck Lutz thanked the impish little man behind the counter and walked to his car.

Once more behind the wheel of his car, with its heater spewing warm air, Lutz radioed headquarters that he had completed the case and would be returning shortly.

He pulled the car into drive and followed the gentle curve of the motel driveway out onto Route 22. Traffic was light, so he quickly eased into the flow headed east on 22 toward Route 66. About a half mile down the road, he passed Joe's Steakhouse and the cornfield.

The slow descent of the crystal globe in Times Square had begun. Its descent signaled a close to the eighth decade of the twentieth century. A decade that began with the invasion of Cambodia and the death of four at Kent State would end with a near nuclear meltdown at Three Mile Island and the invasion of Afghanistan by the Soviet Union. Events of global proportion that shaped our world for years to come can claim their home in the decade that was the 1970s.

For all the hope that a new year brings, especially a new year heralding a new decade, the eve of the dawn of 1980 did not foretell great fortunes or wondrous achievements. In fact, with unemployment at a staggering 5.8 percent and the U.S. steel industry, automobile makers and other members of the industrial complex on the verge of collapse, the promises of 1980 were few and modest.

During the ebbing decade, we had lost the likes of John Wayne, Arthur Fiedler and Nelson Rockefeller to name only a few. Though we could not know it at the time, the new decade would bring the loss of John Lennon, Jean Paul Sartre, the hijacking of the *Achille Lauro*, explosions of the AIDS epidemic and the space shuttle *Challenger* and countless other historic events. For Marlene Sue Newcomer, these impending historic events were but a blip on the horizon on this dawning new year.

For Marlene, the start of 1980 was supposed to mark a new beginning. Several months earlier, her husband had passed away, leaving her alone to care for her son, Jimmy. Alone and with a fatherless six-year-old, Marlene had turned to her friends and family in Leisenring for support.

The eleventh of twelve children, Marlene had recently moved in with her mother, Stella, who was helping to raise young Jimmy. She was just beginning to get back in touch with who she was. Her strong religious conviction had helped guide her through the recent troubled times, and she was once again enjoying singing in the church choir.

What better opportunity to celebrate a new beginning than by ringing in the new year with friends. Celebration brought Marlene into Vandergrift on New Year's Eve 1979. Celebration would cause her path to cross that of Michael Travaglia and John Lesko.

Michael and John spent the nascent hours of 1980 in revelry. While Marlene was sharing festive thoughts with her friends in Vandergrift, Michael and John had joined the Travaglia family for a New Year's Eve celebration at their rural Washington Township home not far from Route 66. Oblivious to the carnage that the younger Travaglia and his partner had left behind, the Travaglia family joined together to welcome in 1980 with hopes for a prosperous new year—hopes that would ultimately fall short.

Satisfied by their brief respite, Lesko and Travaglia set out from the family homestead on foot. The hitchhike back to Pittsburgh was slow going. A thick fog had begun to roll in and the walk was sure to be an unpleasant one. By this time, the temperatures had once again begun to drop into the twenties. Heading toward Route 66, they tucked their hands in the pockets of their jackets and trudged forward.

MARLENE SUE NEWCOMER BECOMES THE SECOND VICTIM

Tuesday, January 1, 1980

Marlene had surprised herself. She had enjoyed her evening in Vandergrift. A small Rockwellian town northeast of Pittsburgh, it seemed as if someone had simply plopped it down at a hairpin turn of the Kiskiminetas River. Sitting on the Westmoreland side of the Westmoreland-Armstrong county line, Vandergrift had once been a busy little town that was home to the steelworkers of George McMurtry's Apollo Iron and Steel Company, but over the years, the population had been dwindling quickly. Many of the mom and pop stores that once lined quaint Grant Avenue were now either closed or on life support.

Even the once thriving Casino Theatre had begun to suffer. Perched at the corner of Grant and Lincoln Avenues in the middle of downtown, it is at the heart of Vandergrift's historic district. The stately theatre, with its four Greek Revival columns, bas-relief Terpsichorean façade and Italian marble flooring, still looked out toward the J&L Steel Rolling Mill on the edge of the river, but these days, the bustle of the mill was gone and the throng of moviegoers had dwindled to a trickle. By late 1979, the theatre, like much of the valley, was slated for demolition.

The twenty-six-year-old seamstress from Connellsville had been reluctant to make the hour drive from her home southeast of Pittsburgh into Vandergrift, but her friends had begged her, and she had finally decided that it would be nice to get out for an evening.

After enjoying the evening with her friends and ushering in the New Year, she said her goodbyes and set out on the forty-five-mile journey back home. The new decade was barely an hour and a half old as Marlene pulled out of the driveway and pointed her car toward Connellsville.

Winding her way down Hancock Avenue, she headed toward Oklahoma Borough. Marlene guided her new Dodge Ramcharger through the deserted streets on the outskirts of Vandergrift. The affable glow of the intermittent streetlights quickly faded in her rearview mirror, and long shadowy pines began to appear like sentinels beside the gray ribbon that snaked its way up and down the hilly countryside. It was dark, and as she maneuvered down Onion Hill toward the river, the gathering fog began to thicken.

Adjusting her headlights, she slowed to a stop at Hancock Avenue and Route 66. Struggling to make out the stop sign at the corner, she hesitated. Finally, confident that it was safe, she turned right onto Route 66 and headed south out of town and toward her home.

Up ahead on the right, trudging along the gravely shoulder just beyond the intersection where Route 356 unites with Route 66, there were two men. As they spun around, thumbs thrust skyward, she slowed to a crawl. Scruffy and cold, their appearance and the fog that swirled around them in the headlights gave them an eerie, ghostlike pallor. It was not in her nature to turn down a stranger in need, and it wasn't something that she was going to start doing now.

Marlene slowed the tan Ramcharger to a crawl and eased it off the asphalt onto the graveled shoulder. Rolling down the window, she shouted, "Come on in out of the fog." One offer was all that was necessary, and the bone-chilled duo rushed to the waiting warmth of Marlene's car.

John opened the door and lifted the front seat for Michael as he climbed into the backseat. With Michael situated, John dropped the seat back into place and quickly climbed into the passenger's side.

"Where are you guys headed?"

"Pittsburgh," offered John.

"Well, I'm headed to Connellsville. I'll take you as far as I can," she replied.

With her passengers safely aboard, Marlene checked through the fog for traffic and then gently pulled back out onto Route 66, once again heading into the night.

Streets with whimsical names like Beaver Run and Poke Run Church Road sprang up through the fog and then slipped back into the night as the three strangers picked their way along the legendary highway of ramblers, dreamers and writers like Jack Kerouac and Woody Guthrie. Snaking through North Washington out past Greensburg Road and Beaver Run Reservoir, the Ramcharger slowly nibbled away at the miles.

Slipping his now thawed hand under his jacket, John toyed with the butt of the .22-caliber revolver. Marlene was concentrating on the foggy highway ahead of her. She was none the wiser. With one swift motion, John drew the gun and pointed it squarely at Marlene.

"Stay calm and you won't get hurt."

Dumbfounded, Marlene was too startled to react—she was too startled to do anything.

"Find a safe place and pull off the road. And don't do anything stupid."

Nervously, Marlene did what her kidnapper ordered and eased off the highway onto the tree-lined gravel shoulder.

"Get in the back," John barked.

Marlene climbed into the backseat beside Michael, who instantly slipped into the front and took her place behind the wheel. Seizing the steering wheel, he gunned the engine and sped back onto Route 66, leaving a trail of sputtering gravel in his wake. Marlene heard the sharp chirp of the tires as the car lurched out onto 66. Into the fog they drove. Michael was in charge of driving. That left John to tend to the new prisoner. Marlene watched him intently as he pulled a long length of yellow wire from under his jacket and reached for her, grabbing her by the arms. Clumsily, he wrapped her wrists with the wire until he was satisfied that she was securely bound. The wire cut deeply into her wrists, but Marlene stifled a cry. She would not let herself cry.

John fumbled around on the backseat until his hand bumped into a wool blanket. It had fallen beside the crevice of the seat as the Ramcharger fishtailed back out onto the highway. With a flourish, he unfurled the blanket and Marlene was plunged into darkness.

As the musty wool blanket settled over her, Marlene thought of funeral shrouds. The darkness under the blanket smothered her. In near panic, she forced herself to focus on the slivers of passing light that intermittently snuck beneath the edge of the blanket. She knew that she had to track where they were headed.

The car lurched to the left and then the right. Marlene guessed Route 286, Saltsburg Road—it had to be. They were headed east out toward Indiana and Beaver Run Reservoir. The path of the Ramcharger once again steadied, and Marlene shifted her efforts to picking out the mumbles of her captors. The two men spoke in low voices. She couldn't make out anything through the thick wool. Fuzzy, garbled syllables and an occasional cackled laugh filtered through, but eventually Marlene gave up trying to hear what they were saying and tried to stay calm. In waves, her fears would creep up on her, nearly overtaking her. She forced them into submission, choosing instead to think of her son.

His pearl-round face smiled at her from beneath a mop of soft, strawberry-blonde hair. Surrounded by piles of newly torn Christmas paper, the smiles and giggles of Christmas morning brought a faint smile to her face. Suddenly, memories of six Christmases past flooded headlong into her brain, crowding out fearful thoughts. With thoughts of future Christmases missed, Marlene Sue Newcomer faded into a world of warm, blue-eyed smiles and toothy grins.

The thunderous roar that erupted as the .22-caliber bullet escaped down the barrel of the gun snapped Marlene back into reality. As the tiny bullet ripped into the fabric of the blanket, a tiny puff of acrid air glanced across her cheek. The bullet whistled past her and lodged harmlessly into the seat just inches from her arm. Her brain raced.

Narrowly missed by the first shot, a second was sure to follow. There would be no second chances. She clutched her chest. Gasping and feigning a heart attack, she played it to the hilt, collapsing opossum-like on the backseat. She prayed that her attackers would fall for her ruse. It had to work.

The tires squealed, and she slid forward against the back of the front seat as the Ramcharger began to swerve back and forth. Sliding left and right, Marlene skidded across the backseat like a hockey puck, and the wool blanket slipped off her and fell onto the floorboards. As quickly as it had begun, the wild gyrations of the car evened out, and they skidded to a stop. Michael whirled in his seat and the interior light came on. She lay motionless, eyes closed, and continued to play dead.

Suddenly she felt an ice-cold hand on her wrist, feeling and groping frantically for a pulse. Her heart was racing. Adrenaline spurted from every pore of her body, but Marlene willed herself to be calm. This would work. This had to work.

Within seconds, the veil of her subterfuge was lifted.

"She's faking it." Marlene opened her eyes to see John's contorted face as he raised the six-inch .22. He slowly drew up the slack in the trigger as his finger curled tighter and tighter around it. Marlene was helpless. Her eyes followed the cylinder as it slowly rotated, pulling another bullet into alignment with the barrel. Slowly, it crept clockwise toward the top, inching into position.

A second thunderous roar rattled the windows in the Ramcharger as hot orange flames reached out and touched her. Searing pain gripped her chest. This was not a miss.

The bullet entered her chest on the left side just above her breast. She felt the warm path of the bullet as it dug into her body. The pain was unlike anything that she had ever experienced. It rushed through her entire body. Every nerve was awake. She had to flee. She could not. All she could do was force her body against the back of the seat and into the corner. Another flash.

She didn't hear the thunderous roar. She didn't hear anything. The tug of the jagged .22-caliber bullet as it tore through the skin on the left side of her head bounced her off the seat. It had entered her skull just above the temple. The muscles in her body recoiled and drove her farther down into the corner of the seat. She was motionless; blood started to drain from the two holes in her body and she could feel it begin to pool beneath her on the seat. There was only silence. Silence and the feel of a scratchy wool funeral shroud once more brushing against her cheek.

Consciousness came and went as they bounded along. As the pool of blood collecting on the floorboards continued to grow, innumerable, incomprehensible thoughts flooded into and out of her head. The reality of her impending death slowly became final. As her heart fluttered and the tiny sparks in her brain darted about, she seized her few remaining threads of strength and slowly but deliberately dipped a cold, pale finger into the pool of blood that had surrounded her. As her finger began to trace a message on the door panel, her frail body shivered and finally gave up. Marlene Sue

Newcomer, beneath her wool shroud, hurtling through Indiana, Pennsylvania, had become John Lesko and Michael Travaglia's second victim.

Oblivious to Marlene's final breaths, the murderous pair raced north on Route 286, once again broke, but now with at least a temporary means of transportation. Michael and John were greeting 1980 with renewed zest. Just ahead, the lights of Indiana, as they mixed with the pale morning sunrise, cast a bluish gray dome of light across the horizon. Michael spotted a convenience store several hundred yards ahead of them in the icy twilight.

Wheeling into the parking lot with Marlene Sue Newcomer's lifeless body draped across the backseat, Michael and John were ready to rock and roll. The two men hopped out of the car and walked into the nearly deserted market. Randy Helman looked up from the newspaper that he had spread across the counter. As John walked toward Helman, he lifted his coat. Sticking out of his waistband was the handgrip of the .22 revolver.

"See this here! I can pull it out in two seconds. Just be calm and you won't get hurt."

As a show of solidarity, Michael lifted his jacket, pulled out a revolver and pointed it at Helman.

"Give us the money," he said.

Randy Helman opened the register and slid what few bills remained in the drawer into the palm of his hand. Casually, he pushed them toward Michael. Michael impatiently clutched at the bills and then crammed them into his pocket. Having emptied the drawer, Randy Helman pushed it closed and looked at John Lesko as if to say, "It's your move."

While Michael was gathering the money, John pulled some yellow electrical wire from his pocket. He walked behind the counter where Helman stood and, working feverishly, wrapped the wire around Helman's wrists. Turn after turn, he wound the wire tighter and tighter. When he had finished with Helman's wrists, he moved to his ankles. He needed to be sure that they would get away. Michael joined him.

Bent industriously over Helman, John and Michael were unaware of Charles Veshinfski, who, while they were busy ordering Helman to the floor, had pulled into the parking lot. It was part of his daily routine—every morning he stopped at the 7-Eleven to buy a paper. On this morning, Charles Veshinfski would not get his paper.

1. The State Correctional Institute at Rockview, located in Centre County Pennsylvania. Rockview is the only correctional institution in Pennsylvania authorized to carry out the death penalty. *Photograph courtesy the Pennsylvania Department of Corrections.*

2. Leonard Miller's senior high school photo, taken circa 1976. *Photograph courtesy Dr. William Kerr.*

3. Indiana University of Pennsylvania's Kiski 1 Regional Police Academy graduating class. Leonard Miller is standing at the center of the back row. *Photograph courtesy James D. Clawson.*

4. Booking photos of John Lesko and Daniel Montgomery. Lesko is pictured on the left, and Montgomery is on the right. *Photograph courtesy the* Valley News Dispatch, *Tarentum, Pennsylvania.*

Above left: 5. Trooper Thomas Tridico, Pennsylvania State Police, shortly after graduation from the State Police Academy, circa 1947. *Photograph courtesy Thomas Tridico.*
Above right: 6. Apollo Borough Police Station as it appears today. Located at 405 North Pennsylvania Avenue, the facility is no longer in use but remains essentially unchanged since January 3, 1980, the night on which Leonard Miller was shot.

7. Joe's Steakhouse, located on Route 22 in Delmont, Pennsylvania, circa 1970. Travaglia and Lesko abandoned Peter Levato's Ford Grenada in the cornfield behind this restaurant on December 27, 1979. *Photograph courtesy Monica Meehan.*

8. Sergeant Thomas Tridico lecturing at the FBI National Academy in Quantico, Virginia, circa 1970. *Photograph courtesy Thomas Tridico.*

9. Thatcher's Motel, located on Route 22 in Delmont, Pennsylvania, as it appears today.

10. Thatcher's Motel, as it appears today.

11. Lobby and office of Thatcher's Motel as they appear today.

Above left: 12. The infamous Edison Hotel still stands at 135 Ninth Street in downtown Pittsburgh, and with the exception of the revamped club in the basement, it has changed very little since the murders in 1979.
Above right: 13. The historic Harris Theatre on Liberty Avenue as it appears today. It is located approximately two blocks from the Edison Hotel, and its appearance is nearly identical to the way it would have looked during the era of Lesko and Travaglia's murder spree.

Above left: 14. The spiraling driveways of the Smithfield-Liberty Parking Garage, where Marlene Sue Newcomer's body was found inside her abandoned Dodge Ramcharger, adjacent to the Gimbels Department Store. The Smithfield-Liberty Garage is located approximately three blocks from the Edison Hotel.
Above right: 15. The sluice gate of the Loyalhanna Dam in rural Westmorland County, Pennsylvania, where Peter Levato was beaten and shot to death.

Above: 16. Looking south from the Loyalhanna Creek bridge at the wooded area where Peter Levato's body was recovered.

Left: 17. The breast of the Blue Spruce Lake Dam. During the winter, the surface of the lake is frozen solid, and the hole through which William Nicholls's body was shoved would have been located approximately twenty-five feet from the concrete retaining wall.

18. North Plaza at the corner of North Astronaut Way and First Street in Apollo as it looks today. On January 3, 1980, Leonard Miller's cruiser was parked in front of the Stop-N-Go (Cogo's today). Travaglia, Lesko and Rutherford sped through this intersection, prompting Leonard Miller to give chase.

19. Cooper Trailer Sales is largely unchanged since Lesko, Travaglia and Rutherford abandoned William Nicholls's Lancia in the parking lot shortly after shooting Leonard Miller on January 3, 1980.

This page, top: 20. William Nicholls's 1977 silver blue Fiat Lancia after the Pennsylvania State Police recovered it on January 3, 1980. *Photograph courtesy the* Valley News Dispatch, *Tarentum, Pennsylvania.*
This page, bottom: 21. The location in which Leonard Miller was gunned down on January 3, 1980. This photo was taken shortly after the murder in 1980, looking east down Route 66 toward Greensburg.

Opposite, top: 22. The location in which Leonard Miller was killed as it appears today. Gianini's Hotel still stands on the right, and Naser's Meat Packing is located directly to the left outside the frame of the photo. This photo was taken looking east on Route 66 toward Greensburg.
Opposite, middle: 23. The location in which Leonard Miller was killed as it appears today, looking northwest toward Apollo, Pennsylvania. Nasar's Meat Packing is visible to the right.
Opposite, bottom: 24. A map depicting the location of Leonard Miller's murder on January 3, 1980. *Illustration courtesy the* Valley News Dispatch, *Tarentum, Pennsylvania.*

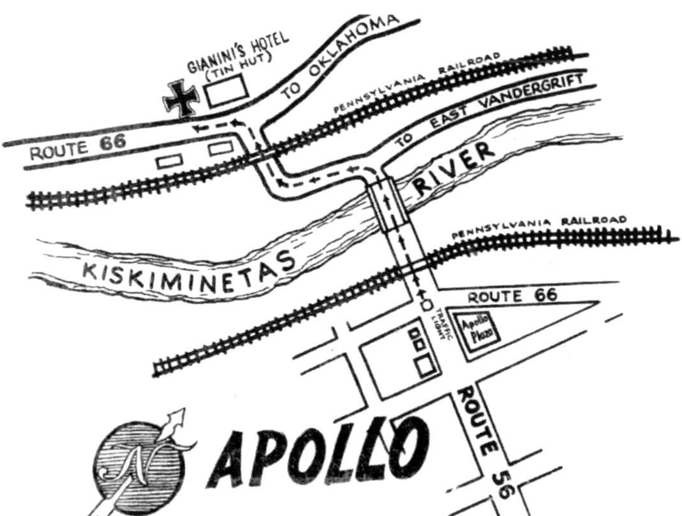

Where murder occurred

25. John Lesko and Michael Travaglia being led from the Westmoreland County Courthouse in handcuffs during their trial in 1981. John Lesko is pictured first, and Michael Travaglia follows. *Photograph courtesy the* Valley News Dispatch, *Tarentum, Pennsylvania.*

26. Leonard Miller's honor guard escorts his body from Curran Funeral Home in Apollo, Pennsylvania, on January 7, 1980. *Photograph courtesy James D. Clawson.*

27. Leonard Miller's honor guard escorts his body to First Lutheran Church in Apollo, Pennsylvania, on January 7, 1980. Pictured from left to right, *front*: Chief Richard Murphy, Officer Charles Sharon and Officer Donald Mahan. *Back*: Officer Robin Davis (obscured), Officer Mark Fetterman and Officer James Clawson. *Photograph courtesy James D. Clawson.*

28. Reverend Zikeli leads Leonard Miller's casket and honor guard down North Pennsylvania Avenue toward the First Lutheran Church. Hundreds of officers line North Pennsylvania Avenue to pay their last respects to Leonard as the honor guard passes. *Photograph courtesy the* Valley News Dispatch, *Tarentum, Pennsylvania.*

29. The First Lutheran Church as it appears today. On the day of Leonard Miller's funeral service, thousands of mourners and more than seven hundred officers crowded the tiny church to pay their last respects.

30. Hundreds of uniformed officers lined the streets of Apollo Borough to pay their respects as Leonard Miller's funeral procession passed by. *Photograph courtesy James D. Clawson.*

31. Leonard Miller's honor guard prepares to load his body into the waiting hearse as a contingent of uniformed officers offer a final salute to their fallen colleague. *Photograph courtesy James D. Clawson.*

32. Leonard Miller's body is loaded into the hearse outside of First Lutheran Church as somber, uniformed officers salute their fallen comrade. Pictured on the left, *front to back*: Officer Donald Mahan, Officer Charles Sharon and Chief Richard Murphy. On the right, *front to back*: Officer James Clawson, Officer Robin Davis and Officer Mark Fetterman. *Photograph courtesy the* Valley News Dispatch, *Tarentum, Pennsylvania.*

This page, top: 33. Reverend Zicelli presides over the graveside interment of Leonard Miller's body. Seated are Evelyn Miller, Frank Miller and an unidentified mourner. *Photograph courtesy the* Valley News Dispatch, *Tarentum, Pennsylvania.*
This page, bottom: 34. Apollo officer Kevin Gibbons sounds Taps as Leonard Miller's body is interred at Riverside Cemetery in Kiski Township, Pennsylvania. *Photograph courtesy James D. Clawson.*

Opposite, top: 35. The Apollo police cruiser that was driven by Leonard Miller on January 3, 1980, the night he was gunned down. *Photograph courtesy James D. Clawson.*
Opposite, middle: 36. Riverside Cemetery as it appears today in Kiski Township, Pennsylvania.
Opposite, bottom: 37. Leonard Miller's well-tended grave, where he is buried with his father, Frank, and mother, Evelyn.

VISITORS

MILLER
LEONARD G.

38. A hand rubbing taken from the granite memorial at the National Police Memorial in Washington, D.C. *Rubbing courtesy James D. Clawson.*

39. The memorial plaque commemorating the dedication of the Apollo Bridge in honor of Leonard Miller.

40. The current Apollo Borough Police shoulder patch. Early in 1979, Leonard Miller himself redesigned the Apollo shoulder patch to incorporate the flying eagle commemorating the Apollo lunar landing. At the time of his death, the patch had not yet been adopted, and shortly after his death, officials added his badge number and issued the shoulder patch as the official insignia of the Apollo Borough Police Department. *Patch courtesy James D. Clawson.*

Part III

Sergeant Tridico Connects the Dots

As he approached the doors, Chuck Veshinfski noticed that something was slightly out of place. Randy, always hovering over his paper at this hour, was nowhere to be seen. Curiosity aroused, Chuck hesitated. As he stood there in the morning twilight, staring through the glass, two suspicious-looking men appeared from behind the counter.

Chuck knew instantly that the scruffy-haired pair must be robbing the place. Remembering the old adage about discretion being the better part of valor, Veshinfski withdrew to the safety of his car. He fumbled in the glove compartment for a piece of paper and started to scribble as fast as he could. The only other car in the store parking lot was a dark brown Ramcharger with a light brown roof and curtains hanging in the side windows. He wrote down the description, tossed the pen and paper on the seat beside him and slipped his car into drive, easing out onto the highway. Chuck Veshinfski drove home, picked up the telephone and called the police. Within minutes, Trooper Michael Steffee was headed toward the 7-Eleven on Route 286.

Wednesday, January 2, 1980, 11:00 p.m.

For Tom Tridico, January 2, 1980, would prove to be a turning point of sorts. For the seasoned investigator, crucial clues would surface today that would help pull together the threads of fabric that would lead him into a head-on confrontation with pure evil.

When he arrived at his office at Troop A headquarters in Greensburg, he did what he did every morning: hung his jacket, poured his coffee and grabbed the log sheet from the day's previous assignments. Settling into his chair, he began to thumb through the list of cases.

He hated being responsible for overseeing investigators. The reports, the paperwork, all of it meant time away from what he loved—investigations. As he ploddingly thumbed through the report, he made mental notes about each case. Some had witnesses; some had no leads at all. If a case had a witness or a lead, he dropped it into a pile marked "follow up." Everything else went into the "inactive" bin. Chuck Lutz's report on the Sonny's Lounge burglary, which he already knew about, landed on the "follow up" pile. Michael Steffee's armed robbery report from the 7-Eleven convenience store landed there too. He continued to the bottom of the pile. After quickly evaluating the last case, he unceremoniously dropped it into the "inactive" bin.

With the daily assignments complete, he got up from his chair and gathered what he would need for the day ahead. He was anxious to meet with Dickey and Boyerinas to discuss their search of Michael Travaglia's repossessed truck. He was sure that what they found would move the Levato case forward. As he threw his coat over his arm and flipped off the light in his office, Tom Tridico saw the frozen face of Peter Levato in the back of his mind.

The weather was gray and overcast. Tom's thirty-minute drive out Route 66 from Greensburg through Mamont, past Beaver Run and into North Washington to the Kiski Valley Barracks gave him time to think. Today was no different from any other day. Thirty degrees and light snow had been the prediction. No snow yet, but the sky was right for it, Tom thought as he rolled through the countryside. Today was no different from any other day.

When Tom arrived at the barracks, Rich Dickey and George Boyerinas were already waiting for him—as usual. Tom walked into the tiny squad room and over to where Dickey was seated. Rich glanced up and then slid a brown paper bag toward him.

"The contents of Travaglia's truck," he said.

Tridico tossed his coat on the back of the closest chair and unfolded the lip of the bag. He dumped the contents on top of the desk: a toy gun, a ski mask, some yellow electrical wire, a set of homemade rope handcuffs and some papers. Picking up the plastic evidence bag containing the wire, his mind reached for the stack of reports in his office. In his mind, he lifted Trooper Mike Steffee's from the top of the pile and examined it.

"Steffee had a robbery yesterday out on 286," he said. "Clerk was tied up with yellow wire."

Tom slid his glasses down on the bridge of his nose for a closer look at the wire: "Carol Cable." He made a mental note to check Steffee's report more closely and then dropped the wire back onto the desktop.

Sifting through the papers, Tridico picked up several, skimming over them: letters, bills, phone numbers. They were an assortment of the details that make up a man's life. As he shuffled through the bits of Michael Travaglia's life, a slip of paper dropped out of the stack and landed on top of the desk.

It was blank except for the name "Ray Scalese" followed by a phone number. Tom studied it for a moment and then raised his eyes toward Rich Dickey. "Check this guy out," he said. Dickey nodded, and Tom dropped the papers back onto the desktop.

Chuck Lutz walked into the squad room to join the other men. Hired back in the days before EEOC (Equal Employment Opportunity Commission), when state troopers were required to be over six feet tall, Chuck was an imposing figure, rough-hewn and rustic, with a full head of salt-and-pepper hair. He dropped his notebook onto a desk and quickly walked toward Tridico and the other men. He thrust a stack of papers toward Tom.

"Arrest warrant for Travaglia," he said, "for the Sonny's Lounge burglary. It'll give us enough to pick him up until we can make him for that Levato thing."

Tridico carefully studied the warrant. Everything seemed to be in order. He handed it back to Lutz. "I'll send out the teletype. Maybe we can round this guy up." Tridico grabbed his coat off the chair and started toward the door. "But right now, I'm heading out to this kid's last known address." He disappeared down the hallway. "I'll let you know what I find." His voice echoed down the hall and faded away.

Tom headed toward the village of Chambers, a collection of middle-class homes spread out over a two- or three-mile patch of land sandwiched between the Beaver Run and Route 66. A mile and a half from Apollo, Chambers sits atop a slight plateau overlooking the Kiskiminetas River. He made a sharp right onto Chambers Street and then slowed his cruiser to a crawl. He looked for street signs.

The few signs that did exist were old and weathered. They offered little help. He crawled along until he reached the end of the road. There was nowhere else to go—it was either right or left. On the northwest corner, he spotted a sign—Fourth Street. He made the right turn and then headed for the only house on the east side of the street.

The Travaglia homestead was purchased in 1960 by Bartolo, Joseph and Bernard Travaglia. It sat slightly off the gravel roadway, crowded up against the tree-covered hillsides that look down on a small ravine cut into the rocky hillside. A winding offshoot of the Kiskiminetas River has carved its way toward the Beaver Run Reservoir, eating away at the hillsides and creating this quaint plateau of ground.

A tidy, two-story structure with a shingle roof, Michael Travaglia's boyhood home sat patiently, waiting and watching, as Tom stepped out of his car and walked along the frosty grass leading to the front door.

Once inside, Tom quickly covered the perfunctory formalities that made up the who, what and why of his visit and then launched gently into a measured series of questions. Tom didn't want to telegraph more details than necessary, but he gently probed the senior Travaglia for vital bits of information that he hoped would bring some closure for Peter Levato.

Bernard Travaglia's wary answers to the questions Tom posed signaled a growing concern over his son's recent behavior. Tom watched Bernard's face flush as he slowly revealed that Michael had owned a .22-caliber handgun. He swallowed hard, paused and, with a hint of hope, said that Michael had been hunting in Ligonier a while back, and a game warden had confiscated the weapon. Tom voraciously scribbled notes. Bernard's voice dropped an octave as he added, "At least that's what Michael said." Tom felt the older man's pain. He was a father, too. He understood how it must have felt for Bernard to slowly realize that his child could be capable of murder.

Tom knew that silence is an interviewer's strongest weapon, so he paused. He waited for that uncomfortable silence to grow so painful that Bernard couldn't let it continue.

"I think he might have taken some electrical cable from my work truck, too," Bernard Travaglia added at last.

Tom was very interested. As Bernard Travaglia's wavering voice dropped the rest of the bits of information one at a time, Tom scribbled the words "Carol Cable" on the bottom corner of his notebook in big letters.

Whether the hardworking patriarch of the Travaglia family fully grasped the gravity or significance of the information he had just given the affable investigator was unclear to Tom. What was clear is that those seemingly innocuous strands of random data bounced around in Tom's head all the way back to the barracks. He knew that he was tracking the right man.

That evening, with the winter sun well below the horizon, Tom Tridico sat in his living room clearing away the jagged details of his day. The monotone voices of velvet baritone newscasters rattled off the highlights and lowlights of another average Steel City day, and Tom drifted in and out of a light slumber. Filtered words bounded around in his head, and the flicker of images that crept through his half-open eyelids washed over him without effect.

Suddenly, one sharp word poked his amygdalae, jolting his eyes open. The word was "murder." By the time Tom cleared the fog from his eyes, the news anchor had handed off the story to a shivering field reporter positioned strategically in front of a yellow ribbon of police barrier tape draped in front of the swirling circular ramps of the Smithfield Liberty garage. Now fully engaged, Tom drank in every detail.

As the velvet-draped body rolled behind him on a rickety gurney, the frozen reporter recounted the details of the recovery of a woman's body from the third floor of the Gimbel's Department Store parking garage downtown. "Shot twice with a small caliber handgun, police speculate that the motive for the killing is robbery," the reporter said. Tom heard nothing more; he only saw. Sitting in the background of the frame, surrounded by evidence technicians and police detectives, Marlene Sue Newcomer's new Dodge Ramcharger—two-tone brown with window curtains—screamed at him, "Look at me." He scrambled from his chair and reached for the phone.

As he dialed the phone, his mental checklist rattled off to-do items at a mile a minute. Eventually, after working his way through the phone bureaucracy, he heard the voice of Sergeant John Flannigan, night supervisor for the Pittsburgh Police Department's homicide squad, on the other end.

"Sergeant Flannigan, this is Sergeant Tom Tridico, PSP out of Greensburg," Tom began as his mind started to equalize. "I think I might have some information on that body recovery you had out at the Gimbel's parking lot this morning."

As the two bosses exchanged information and began to align the details of their respective cases, it became more and more clear to Tom Tridico that Michael Travaglia and his partner were not only responsible for the murder of Peter Levato, but also for that of Marlene Sue Newcomber and possibly numerous other armed robberies. These are very bad men, Tom decided.

After their brief conversation, Tridico and Flannigan agreed that meeting in person would be best. They set an appointment for 9:30 a.m. the following morning at the downtown headquarters of the Pittsburgh Public Safety Department. Tom Tridico would not make it to the meeting.

Michael hated Doggone Sam's hotdog shop. The tiny eatery always stunk of onions, stale bread and fresh Pine-Sol. He tried not to breathe through his nose. The fidgety fluorescent bulbs overhead washed the dingy little shop in bile-green coolness. It reminded him of Halloween. The swirling snowflakes outside the window threw themselves against the glass and then leapt into the night sky, oblivious to the men inside hatching plans of murder and robbery. Michael Travaglia had full control of the meeting. John and fifteen-year-old Ricky Rutherford sat in studied contemplation as Michael laid out the new plan.

Earlier in the day, Michael and John had stopped at the Smithfield Street arcade long enough for Michael to drop the last of Marlene Sue Newcomers quarter's into a game of *Galaxian*. Ricky was already leaning against one of the machines when the men strolled in, and he insisted that they let him tag along. Michael didn't have a good feeling about Ricky, but the kid had been so persistent that he figured what could it hurt? Michael knew he would regret it.

Michael preferred that his partners had only as much information as they needed, so he figured that his concise instructions to "wait outside in the alley" were plenty and abruptly adjourned the meeting. With a nod of agreement, the men stood up from the table and then hustled out the side door.

Pushing headlong into the cold, the men headed down Ninth Street toward the Edison Hotel. The familiar brown weathered stones of the Edison loomed a few hundred feet farther down Ninth Street. Tiny squalls of snow scattered under Michael's feet as they walked quickly in the direction of French Street. Michael's new plan had energized them. When they reached the front door of the Edison Hotel, Michael peeled off from the other two men and disappeared inside.

BILL NICHOLLS BECOMES THE THIRD VICTIM

John and Ricky continued halfway down the street and then ducked into the darkened alley behind the Edison, where they waited in frozen silence. As the minutes crept by, Ricky nervously moved about, trying to stave off the chill that permeated the January night. Trying to keep warm, he banged his hands together. It didn't help.

"It must be an hour already," he mumbled to himself. John turned to him, "When you see a car coming down the alley and hear a horn beep, that will be Mike."

Ricky nodded and then went back to banging his hands together. He wiggled his toes in his shoes to try and get the feeling back. That didn't help either. His feet were frozen chunks of flesh, and he was starting to regret begging so hard. The idle of an engine crept up behind him and he spun around.

Bill Nicholls sat proudly behind the wheel of his new silver blue Lancia. He had been the proud owner of the new sports car for all of eighteen hours, and he was eager to show it off to his new friend. As they pulled into the alley behind the Edison Hotel, Michael reached over and tapped the horn. Bill thought this was a bit odd but didn't give it a second thought—not until the two figures bounded from the shadows toward his car.

The passenger door flew open and John hurled himself inside the car. Bill was too busy watching the scruffy, disturbing man climbing into his backseat to see Michael slip the .22 revolver from his jacket.

Bill felt the sting of the bullet before he heard anything. It took him quite by surprise. The bullet screamed through Bill's arm. It ripped into his flesh, and he jerked his body back against the seat. All he heard was the ruckus created by John and Ricky clamoring into the car. They drowned out Bill's shrill screams of pain.

"How did it sound? Was it loud?" Michael asked as John and Ricky clumsily piled in.

"It sounded like a firecracker," said John.

Bill Nicholls writhed in pain as blood poured from the soft flesh of his right bicep and quickly began to soak the sleeve of his jacket. "Get in the back." Michael ordered as he shoved Bill toward the backseat, where John had already settled in. Michael slid behind the wheel, and Ricky jumped into the passenger 's seat. Moments later the three men and their captive were speeding down Penn Avenue, headed out of town and into the darkness.

As the car hurtled along, darting in and out of the snowy hillsides along Route 119 headed toward Indiana, John Lesko began to torment the injured man in the backseat. Already handcuffed and bleeding heavily, Bill tried hard to defend himself from John's meaty fists as they crashed into his body. He could not stop the beating.

Eventually, Bill surrendered to his attacker's onslaught and collapsed, exhausted, against the backseat. Undaunted by Bill's submission, John continued laughing and taunting the bleeding man. Harder and harder he drove his fists into his victim as Bill drifted in and out of consciousness. Again and again John hit him, each blow harder than the last. Bill couldn't escape the pain.

With every fist fall, the shrieks of pain that exploded from his wounded arm drove Bill Nicholls closer and closer to unconsciousness. Drifting back and forth between lucidity and stupor, Bill could feel his bloody and broken body slowly dropping into unconsciousness.

Illuminated by only the eerie green fluorescence of the dashboard lights, the three men and their victim rocketed along the winding country highways for what seemed like an eternity. After an hour and a half of inflicting brutality on the semiconscious Bill Nichols, the bright lights of the Steel City were far behind them. Michael veered off Route 119 onto Route 110. A mile past Grove Chapel Road, there was a tiny, unmarked road that wound off into the darkness.

The silver blue Lancia turned off Route 110 onto Blue Spruce Road and skidded to a halt. Michael Travaglia glanced in his rearview mirror and then sat for a moment. Confident that no one was following them, he gunned the engine. The car jerked forward like a shot back out onto the road.

As the car picked up speed, tiny swirling snowflakes began to dance along the highway in little pirouettes and then threw themselves underneath the speeding car. Coaxing the car along the gently winding road, Michael regripped the wheel and then glanced out into the dark woods. The surreal landscape hurtling past them in the inky black night was familiar to him. The monotonous thrum of the drilling machinery and the acrid aroma of natural gas had worked into his brain, poking and prodding it, catapulting him back in time fifteen years until he was once more sitting in the backseat of the family car as they drove out toward the family cabin on Blue Spruce Lake.

Dragging himself back into the present, Michael shifted in his seat and refocused on what he had to do. William was silent. The bitter odor of burning gunpowder, singed flesh and warm blood still filled the cabin of the car, and Michael pushed harder on the gas pedal.

He knew this road by heart and mindlessly pushed on to his destination. In the distance, the faint amber glow of the Lakeside Center Pavilion caught his eye. Nervously, he scanned the parking lot for any signs of life. In warmer times, it was not uncommon for young lovers to steal away to the shores of this secluded lake hoping to find eternal love among the whispering pines—tonight there was no one. Relieved, he raced headlong around the next curve.

A throaty baritone moan escaped from the slender, pale lips of the semi-comatose prisoner in the back. John spun around in his seat and slammed a meaty fist square into the bridge of Bill's nose. Bill's body quivered and then gently slumped over against the door.

The sliver of moon that hung in the sky cast an eerie, wandering shadow onto the lake as the headlights of the Lancia rounded the last curve in the road. Shapeless demons danced and pursued one another in the night, playing their fiendish game of cat and mouse across the lake's icy surface. Mesmerized and pumped with adrenaline, Michael watched the headlights devour the gravely gray pavement leading up to the lakeside.

He nearly missed the turnoff. Michael jerked the wheel hard to the right and sent the car skidding onto the gravely surface of Groft Road. As he hit the gas, rocks and stones scattered into the underbrush. The abrupt turn sent the tail end of the car into a wide arc, and Michael struggled hard to control the vehicle. Fishtailing this way and that on the loose gravel, the car began to spin out of control. Quickly correcting the spin, Michael finally pulled the car under control and headed down the middle of the dusty, narrow road.

Two hundred yards ahead, barely visible in the moonlight, the familiar shapes of the pavilions surrounding the main parking lot of the lake began to take shape. The solitude of Blue Spruce Lake was perfect for what they had to do. Darting past the large, open parking lot, Michael slowed the car to a crawl and began to creep as close to the lake's shore as he could get. Satisfied that he could go no farther, he switched off the ignition.

A cold seclusion enveloped the car. The only sounds inside the car were the slow, measured breaths of the three conscious men intermittently punctuated by a frail moan of the semiconscious backseat passenger. Outside the car, the night sounds of winter filtered through the piney woods. The sharp, crisp cracks made by the shifting ice on the lake sporadically disrupted the still silence of the woods. They sat motionless. Then, without a word, the three men bailed from the car.

The rush of arctic air that filled the cockpit of the Lancia as Ricky threw the passenger's door open breathed a spark of life into Bill Nicholls, and he began to struggle against the bindings on his hands. He screamed for help.

Michael, John and Ricky grabbed Bill by the shoulders and dragged him out of the car. As the men struggled with the thrashing man, long, slender shadows danced around them on the gravel. Pushing and shoving, they finally freed Bill's body from the car. He dropped onto the frozen ground and continued his struggle. John pounced on the bloody and frantic captive. A flurry of fists began to rain down on William Nicholls. Blow after blow pushed him further and further into nothingness. When Bill's struggles finally subsided, John hovered over his limp victim, drawing long, frozen breaths into his winded lungs. Standing in silence, the three men stared down into the now inanimate face of William Nicholls.

Without a word, Michael turned and headed off toward the frozen lake, and John and Ricky began working on Bill Nicholls in silence. Jerking Nicholls's belt from around his waist, John wrapped it around his ankles and then tied it tightly. Ricky scurried around the rocky bank gathering up as many stones and loose rocks as he could carry. With arms heaped full of rocks, he trotted back to the car.

The two men then forced the odd-shaped pieces of limestone into the jacket and pants pockets of the dying man. Stuffing his pockets and jacket until lopsided lumps and bulges protruded from every angle, they furiously tried to add weight to his body. In the distance, from out on the ice, sharp rhythmic sounds began to echo off the tree line as Michael hacked and chopped through the six-inch sheet of ice, his frozen fingers wrapped around a large piece of jagged limestone.

John and Ricky rolled Bill onto his back. They unzipped his jacket and continued shoving large rocks into it until it could hold no more. When it was filled, John struggled and tugged until finally the straining and distorted zipper of Bill's jacket finally crept up, sealing thirty pounds of ballast inside.

The slushy sounds of Michael's chopping faded into the trees, and the *click-clack* of his shoes on the ice grew louder. Michael skated off the ice and rushed to his waiting partners. He knelt down to inspect the body. The icy winds whipping across Blue Spruce Lake bit at his fingers, and he rubbed his hands together briskly. Not much better. What he had expected to take five minutes felt like it had taken an hour. His hands were frozen. He cursed Bill Nicholls under his breath for being difficult.

He motioned for John and Ricky. Together, the two men seized Bill's shoulders and began pushing. Michael started pulling at the body as hard as he could. With John and Ricky holding onto Bill's clothing, all three dark figures pulled, struggled and tugged, until the body began to inch toward the smooth sheet of ice covering the lake. Slowly it slid inch by inch out onto the ice. Once out on the ice, the body began to slide more easily. Foot by foot, they slid him farther out, closer and closer to the waiting hole. When the men reached the three-foot gaping hole in the ice, they all stood up. Michael breathed a sigh of relief.

The three men stood motionless near the west end of the lake. They were about twenty-five yards from the breast of the dam. Bill Nicholls's unconscious body lay at their feet about three feet from a watery grave.

John smiled an evil-looking smile, perfected over years of abuse, and drew in a long breath. He exhaled a long, frosty breath and began to push the body toward the waiting hole in the ice with his foot. Michael's heart raced. Two more shoves and Bill Nicholls's body teetered on the brink of the hole.

John placed the heel of his boot on William Nicholls's shoulder and then looked at Michael. Michael smiled. John gave the unconscious body one last push. The icy water of Blue Spruce Lake returned William Nicholls into the world of the conscious and triggered violent shrieks and screams. Sounds of his frantic struggle echoed off the gray concrete dam as he plunged feet first into the gaping darkness.

Then there was nothing—no splash—nothing more than icy silence as the weighted body disappeared into the black water. Suddenly, the surface of the water churned and boiled. William Nicholls's head broke the surface and his body began thrashing about violently. Hands, tied with heavy yellow wire, began clawing and grasping at the jagged edges of the icy hole, desperately trying to find a handle. As William Nicholls's head bobbed on the surface of the water, the three men looked at one another in astonishment. Michael had not anticipated that Bill would struggle. In a flurry of angry obscenities and epithets, John began thrusting his foot downward onto the top of the thrashing man's head. He kicked again and again, each time bringing his foot down harder and harder. Water and blood-tinged ice flew through the air. Michael and Ricky joined in. Repeatedly, the men drove their heels into the bleeding and crushed skull of William Nicholls, until his water-filled lungs could no longer offer any resistance. Then, as suddenly as it had begun, it ended. The water grew calm and still. Silence blanketed the tree-rimmed lake again, and all that remained of the gruesome murderous rampage were the measured, heavy breaths of the exhausted murderers. The three men stood silently beside the hole, and then one by one, without a word, they turned toward the silver blue Lancia and calmly walked off the ice.

The Fourth Victim Is Claimed

Thursday, January 3, 1980, 3:00 a.m.

The Fiat's engine clattered as it sparked to life, breaking the stranglehold of the desolate silence that had engulfed them. The oppressive darkness surrounding the sports car retreated into the trees as the furious headlamps burst out into the night. Michael slowly rubbed his hands, trying to get the feeling back in his fingers. He gripped the wheel tightly and stared intently at the tiny red specks of William Nicholls's flesh on his knuckles. In the dim dome light of the car's interior, he smiled a crooked, curved, evil little smile.

The third murder was done. In the space of fewer than four hours, these three deranged men had abducted, tortured and killed, in a most gruesome and cruel manner, a stranger—the third stranger in a murderous rampage that had begun only five days earlier.

As the tires rattled across the iron grating of the bridge, Michael reached down and ran his thumb across the checked surface of the wooden handgrip on the .38-caliber revolver that the three men had just stolen from Bernard Travaglia's truck. His new firepower reassured him, and he began to imagine how the gun was going to feel when he squeezed the trigger. The black-and-white police cruiser parked in the plaza lot next to the Stop-N-Go brought Michael back to reality.

Ricky spotted the cop car first. "How are we going to rob the place with that cop hanging out there?" he asked.

"Relax. Let's have some fun with this guy. We'll get him to chase us, and when we get him out of town, we'll come back and rob the place," Michael answered.

The plan seemed logical enough. Michael gave the car some gas and headed toward the intersection of Astronaut Way and First Street. Ignoring the red signal, Michael floored the accelerator and careened through the intersection, then flew past the idling Apollo police cruiser. Climbing the hill, the trio waited for the flashing lights—there were none.

As it dawned on them that no police pursuit was imminent, Michael wheeled the car around and headed back down the hill into town once again. This time Michael's speed topped eighty miles per hour. As he accelerated into the intersection, he began blowing the horn. The car lurched through the intersection, and to the delight of the three men, red and blue flashes signaled the promise of a chase.

As Michael flew across the bridge, the headlights of Leonard Miller's patrol car appeared in his rearview mirror. John Lesko leaned toward Ricky. "Lay down in the back," he said. "This is going to turn into a shooting gallery."

Ahead on the right, the dilapidated Gianinni's Hotel slumbered behind weathered, white-chalk wooden siding. Satisfied that they were beyond the Armstrong County line and thus beyond the limits of the Apollo Police Department's jurisdiction, Michael abruptly skidded the Lancia to a stop. Barely pulling off the highway before stopping, Michael looked in the rearview mirror and saw the police cruiser's headlights closing fast.

As the headlights angled in behind him, Michael pulled the silver snub-nosed revolver from his waistband and rested it against the door, just below the edge of the window.

Leonard Miller's body cast long, dancing shadows inside of the stolen Lancia as the patrol car's door swung open and he stepped out. Michael watched the shadows in the mirror as Leonard lifted his nightstick from the seat beside him and slid the solid oak shaft into the metal ring hanging from the left side of his duty belt. The solid clack of wood against the metal ring echoed off the siding of Nasar's Meat Packing House down along the river and bounced off Michael's ear. Leonard adjusted his gun belt, steadied his round felt campaign hat and strode toward the idling silver blue sports car.

Michael listened intently to the quickly approaching footsteps. Each scrape of leather against pavement brought Leonard Miller one step closer to uncovering their reign of terror. With William Nicholls's wallet and belongings in the glove box and the .22-caliber pistol they had used to kill

Peter Levato and Marlene Sue Newcomer tucked into John Lesko's waist, it would only be a matter of time before their killing spree was undone. The steady *slip-clap* of Leonard Miller's strides grew louder. Michael slid his thumb onto the knurled edge of the .38's hammer. Easing it back, he felt the click of the action as the cylinder rotated into position, chambering a single .38-caliber bullet. Miller's ample frame walked around the driver's side of the car and stepped into the doorway, casting a large, looming shadow over the occupants.

Michael's fingers twitched as he slowly raised the gun. He slowly squeezed the trigger until the roar of 158 grains of lead rocketing from the two-inch gun barrel jolted him backward. As the first bullet entered Leonard Miller's body, Michael heard John in the passenger seat screaming, "Shoot him again, shoot him again!" Michael choked on the smoke as it filled the cabin. Leonard Miller dropped to one knee on the pavement outside Michael's door, and Michael squeezed the trigger again, sending a second slug screaming into Leonard as he recoiled from the car door.

Smoke and unburned powder hung in the air outside the car window where Leonard Miller fell backward. Grasping at the police revolver that dangled in the holster by his side, his training took over, and he drew his weapon. Stumbling backward onto the pavement, Leonard began to fire. Squeezing again and again, he sent bullet after bullet in the direction of Michael, John and Ricky. The first struck the side window and sent a shower of glass raining down on them. Michael felt the sting of blood in his eye. Stunned that Leonard had returned fire, he panicked. Michael slammed the car into drive and crushed the gas pedal.

Thick black stripes of rubber appeared under the tires of the Lancia as it accelerated south on Route 66. Leonard continued firing, sending the last of his six bullets into the rear passenger's side quarter panel of the car as it disappeared down the road. As the taillights rapidly vanished into the darkness, Leonard reholstered his gun and collapsed onto the cold, gray pavement.

The first round had struck Leonard in the abdomen; the second had found its mark in his shoulder. From both pencil-sized holes, growing crimson blobs began to engulf his shirt. As the blood rapidly drained from his body, Leonard began crawling back toward his idling cruiser. Covering the twenty-five feet took every ounce of strength that remained in his 250-pound body. When he reached the open door, he searched for the microphone that he had left lying on the seat.

Once he found it, Leonard wrapped his thick, blood-covered hand around the microphone and depressed the button. "RC-70 to Control. 10-13." Leonard gasped for breath. "They shot me. They shot me twice…come out to the West Apollo slaughterhouse—" Leonard's voice trailed off as his body dropped onto the pavement beside his black and white, microphone still clasped in his hand.

Donald Mahan had been working the evening shift in Apollo Borough on January 2. When Leonard arrived for his shift that night, Donny handed over the keys to the car, briefed him on the events of the evening and said goodbye. From there, Donny made the five-minute drive across the Kiskiminetas River to Vandergrift, where he would spend the next eight hours as a Vandergrift police officer. Neither man knew that their goodbyes would be their last.

When Donny Mahan heard Leonard Miller's call for help, he and his partner, fellow Vandergrift veteran Lou Purificato, knew immediately that Miller's situation was dire. His speech, garbled and distant, sounded as if he were underwater. When his initial transmission was inaudible, the dispatcher asked him to repeat it, but Leonard's voice faded away. Mahan and Purificato wasted no time running to Miller's side. Flying down McKinley Avenue onto Sheridan Road, which ran alongside the river toward Route 66, the two Vandergrift officers took the back route to Apollo and reached Leonard within two minutes of his fateful call for help.

When they arrived, Lou Purificato and Donny Mahan found Leonard barely breathing and lying face down in a pool of blood. Everything around Leonard Miller was covered in blood, and the officers immediately began valiantly trying to save their dying colleague. Most of Leonard's blood had spilled from his body, and despite their tireless efforts, it was too late. Leonard Miller never regained consciousness, and within moments, Lou Purificato and Donald Mahan were huddled over the lifeless body of their friend and colleague. Silence—cold, crisp and forever—gripped the west end of the Apollo Bridge. The light snow that had begun to fall seemed to hang in the air, as if fearful of touching down on the hallowed ground where

Leonard's lifeless body lay. Instead, it swirled, danced and hovered just above the ground.

Leonard Miller, the only child of Frank and Evelyn Miller, was dead. His lifelong dream, realized for only three short days, had claimed him in the midst of doing what he loved. His sacrifice, felt deeply by the two men who were with him to the last, would ripple throughout the valley for the next twenty-nine years. As the news of Leonard's death began to spread, the town awoke to a haze of disbelief and sorrow. No words will ever heal the wounds felt by this close-knit community; nor will justice ever truly come for those who knew and loved Leonard Miller. He was gone, and nothing, not even Donald Mahan and Lou Purificato, could bring him back. Michael Travaglia and John Lesko had claimed their fourth victim and disappeared into the night without a trace.

At 4:50 a.m., the harsh, shrill ringing of his telephone startled Tom Tridico awake. For veteran investigators such as Tridico, a 5:00 a.m. phone call is neither unexpected nor unusual. The call that Tom received this morning was both. In the career of a police officer, few phone calls are dreaded more. The news of the murder of a fellow officer strikes both deep and hard—in part because not only has a comrade made the ultimate sacrifice, but also because, in some small way, it serves as a cold reminder of one's own mortality. After gathering the details and hanging up the phone, Tom numbly dressed and headed out to the scene.

The freezing drive—made even colder by its purpose—from Tom's home in Greensburg to the outskirts of Apollo took him forty-five minutes. On the seat beside him lay a photo of Michael Travaglia. When he arrived at the scene, the cluster of firefighters, EMS personnel and police officers was surreal. He struggled to focus and knew that as tough as what he was about to do was, he owed it to Leonard Miller.

As he stepped from his unmarked car and walked toward the group, he saw the lifeless body of fellow officer Leonard Miller. Trooper Robert Luniewski was one of the stunned crowd huddled around Leonard's body. Tom recognized him immediately and approached. He put aside his own grief and fears and began the most difficult investigation of his career.

Tom walked the scene with Bob Luniewski, making notes and directing Trooper Marshall to photograph this and mark that for reference. In his mind, he was working any other murder, just like the two hundred cases he had worked before—methodical, clinical and professional. In his heart, he was dying.

Tom sketched the location of the tire tracks in his notebook, and a sharp glint from something lying in the roadway caught his eye. He walked over to where the tracks began. As he bent down, the light from the dozen or so police cars that encircled the scene danced and flashed off several shards of broken glass lying in the highway.

Tom called Trooper Rick Marshall over. As crime scene photographer, Tom had worked with Rick hundreds of times before. Without a word from Tom, Marshall raised his bulky Speed Graphic to his eye and snapped some pictures. The flashes popped, shooting milky blue light out one hundred yards in all directions, and Tom blinked his eyes. No matter how many times he did this, he always forgot about the flashes.

After Rick took two pictures, Tom placed a brown paper evidence bag beside the glass, and, instinctively, Rick took several steps back to get a wider shot. Tom appreciated working with Rick. Rick understood the fundamentals of crime scene photography, and Tom couldn't remember a single time that he had to remind him to get wide, medium and close-up photos of his evidence. Rick was a good trooper.

When Rick nodded to Tom, he knew that it was safe for the crime scene unit to begin collecting the shards of glass and he moved on. A theory began to emerge, and he mulled it over in his head as he began walking toward Leonard's body. Tom had consciously avoided this since he had arrived, but he knew that his investigation wouldn't be complete until he examined Leonard. Tom Tridico was nothing if not complete.

When Tom knelt beside Leonard's body, every fiber of his two-hundred-pound, middle-aged frame ached. Lying on the cold, hard pavement was one of his own. Separating Leonard Miller, fallen police officer, gunned down in cold blood, from Leonard Miller, the first homicide victim of 1980, was almost impossible. But Tom Tridico knew that there would be no closure for Leonard if he didn't make that separation. Tom swallowed hard, placed his emotions in a tiny box, slid them high onto a shelf and closed the door. Tom was ready to examine Leonard's body.

Tom suspected that the glass on the highway was from the suspect's car. If that were the case, it had probably come from a gunfight between Leonard and his assailant. Tom gingerly unholstered Leonard's service revolver. The blue steel Smith & Wesson was ice cold. Tom scratched a tiny mark on the cylinder to later identify its location and then slid the thumb catch. He gently flicked his wrist and popped the cylinder out. Six tiny dimples stared back at him. Tom smiled slightly. Leonard had not gone quietly into the night. Tom flipped the cylinder closed and then glanced over his shoulder. Rick's slight nod told him everything he needed to know, and Tom handed the revolver off to the crime scene technicians for processing.

The tiny holes in Leonard's body were almost invisible. In fact, if it hadn't been for the massive pool of blood surrounding Leonard, one might almost miss them. It had always amazed Tom how much carnage two tiny holes no bigger than a number two pencil could make. The hole in Leonard's abdomen would probably prove to be the fatal shot, but Tom knew that was the medical examiner's call. He glanced at the silver shield lying on Leonard's chest. Tom Tridico locked the closet door of his emotions and then stood up.

Tom scanned the scene. He had photographed, sketched and begun collecting what little evidence there was. Not much left to do here, he thought. As he stood there in the growing light of dawn, a fine dusting of snowflakes began to float down from the sky. Without a word, Tom walked to his car. He grabbed a blanket from his trunk and clumsily unfolded it. As he walked toward Leonard's body, the anger in his stomach began to creep up into the back of his throat. When he reached Leonard, he gently draped the blanket over him. He pretended it was to protect the scene.

Tom hesitated, inhaled deeply to force the bile back down into his stomach and made a silent promise to Leonard. After a moment of standing there in desolate isolation, a fellow investigator gently tapped his shoulder. He had discovered two possible witnesses to the shooting. Tom's moment of silence was over.

Sergeant Tridico Vows to Find the Killers

Linda McLaughlin and Thomas Bodnar had been standing in the plaza parking lot when Michael Travaglia and his passengers sailed through the traffic signal at First Street and Astronaut Way. They had seen Leonard speed across the bridge after them and then they had heard the gunfire. Tom Bodnar had raced to the middle of First Street and stared off into the frozen darkness on the other side of the bridge, trying to see what had happened. But two hundred yards and the veil of night had conspired against him, and he couldn't even see Leonard Miller's headlights. Sensing that there was something desperately wrong, Bodnar ran back to the Stop-N-Go and grabbed the phone to call for help. Other than that, neither Bodnar nor McLaughlin had much information. What they did have was a description of the car. They described a late model, silver blue sports car occupied by several men. This information would provide Tom Tridico with what he needed to send out an all-points bulletin to police departments in the area asking for assistance in the search for the killers.

When Tom arrived back at the barracks, he sorted through the information that had begun pouring in since news of the slaying had spread moments after the shots were fired. Investigative triage was a skill that Tom had perfected early in his career. It had helped him earn his stripes. The physical evidence was scant. A few fragments of glass, plenty of blood—which appeared to belong solely to Officer Miller—and little else. He wished for more but had made cases on less, so he didn't lose hope. He knew that ballistic evidence would prove helpful, but recovery of the bullets from Leonard Miller's body wouldn't happen until several hours later, so he focused on the information that he did have.

If Miller's defensive shots had struck his killer, then there were no obvious signs of it at the scene. Of course, that didn't rule out the possibility that he had, in fact, wounded his assailant, but there were no traces of blood left behind. Tom was getting ready to notify the local hospitals just in case when he was interrupted.

When Tom stepped into the barracks' lobby at 7:15 a.m., Ronald Ashton met him with eager anticipation. Ashton wanted desperately to help. He had been on his way to work, heading out Route 380, when he noticed a silver blue sports car parked off the side of the road. Tom held his breath. Ashton had heard the description of the car on his police scanner that morning while he was getting ready for work. Tom thanked his stars for police buffs. The car looked like it had a couple bullet holes in it, Ashton offered. That was all that Tom needed to hear. He immediately signaled for one of the dozen or so troopers milling around expectantly looking for things to do to come take the statement from Ashton and then snatched up his coat and headed to his car.

After Tom had settled in behind the wheel of his police-issue unmarked car, he radioed for Troopers David Ivey and Steven Szabo, who were patrolling the area, to head to Coopers Trailer Sales out on Route 380 to investigate. Optimistically, Tom dropped the car into gear and headed out to meet them.

Within five minutes of their arrival, Szabo and Ivey radioed to Tom that they had hit the jackpot. Tom goosed the police car and held his breath. This would be the break they needed, he could feel it.

By 7:30 that morning, Tom Tridico was standing beside a half dozen state troopers surveying a 1977 silver blue Fiat Lancia. Tridico closed down the entrances to the lot with several uniformed officers stationed at each end. While waiting for Rick Marshall, Tom began a quick once over of the car. He noted two bullet holes in the passenger's side quarter panel. No doubt the slugs would match Leonard's gun.

The driver's window was shattered, and tiny little fragments of safety glass littered the seats. Tom wasn't a gambler, but if he were a betting man, he'd have bet his house, impending pension and his daughters' college funds on the glass fragments matching those he had found at the crime scene.

Taking a step back from the car, Tom collected his thoughts and began to plan his next step. Unless the killers had stolen another car or hitched a ride, they couldn't have gotten too far. Hopeful, Tom radioed to his patrol units in the area instructing them to begin canvassing along Route 380. He knew that if he was going to track Leonard's killer down, he needed all the help he could get. He had the barracks pass along everything he knew up to this point to the police in the surrounding towns of Plum Borough, Murrysville and Monroeville. Tom knew that more eyes were always a good thing.

Tom didn't have to ask twice. Troopers, local police and county detectives fanned out across the three counties searching for the cop killers. In reality, Tom hadn't really had to ask at all. From the moment the news of Leonard's murder hit the airwaves, cops from every tiny town and borough in a three-county area had been going inch by inch over the countryside, sifting through everything in hopes that something would surface that would reveal Leonard Miller's killer.

At 10:00 a.m., the police saturation paid off. As part of the dragnet, Trooper Frank Sheetz had been assigned to canvass along 380. Route 380 is a main artery running through the small town of Holiday Park on the outskirts of Monroeville. As a back route to Pittsburgh, it is pretty well travelled and dotted with convenience stores, gas stations and shopping plazas. Trooper Sheetz hadn't gotten more than a five-minute walk from the Cooper Trailer Sale's parking lot when he reached the 7-Eleven convenience store.

The night manager at the store remembered three strange men at the store around 7:00 a.m. that morning. One of the men had a small cut above his eye, and they were all acting a bit suspicious. Asking the clerk and customers for a ride into Pittsburgh, the men had apparently run into an acquaintance and then disappeared. He couldn't be sure, but it sounded to the clerk as if the men were headed into McKeesport, or maybe Elizabeth. The man with the cut was described as tall and lean with straggly brown hair and scruffy facial hair. Immediately, Sheetz radioed to Tom Tridico, who sent George Boyerinas and Rich Dickey to the store with the photograph of Michael Travaglia. Dickey showed the photo. The clerk never hesitated. Michael Travaglia was the man with the cut above his eye.

Within minutes, Tom Tridico was on the phone with the McKeesport Police. Chief Thomas Hanna was on the other end. The camaraderie that emerges among agencies in a time of such crisis is what makes the subculture of the police community such a tightknit group. Eager to do anything within his power, Tom Hanna pledged all his men and resources to aid in the search. Armed with a description of the three men and a photograph of Michael Travaglia, Troopers Sheetz and Griffin set out to join Tom Hanna and his men as they scoured the rusty streets and alleys of McKeesport for three scruffy and deadly men.

Having dispatched men to all parts of Westmoreland, Allegheny and Armstrong Counties, setting a record-breaking dragnet in motion, Tridico returned to the Kiski Valley Barracks. He sat at a tiny, overcrowded desk running through facts, checking off bits of evidence in his head and staring at the face of Michael Travaglia in his mind. He had done all that he could do. The case was in the hands of his men in the street. He had faith in them. Feeling helpless, Tom reached across the desk, lifted the receiver from its cradle and mashed the stout buttons on the keypad with his tired fingers.

John Flannigan's voice reminded Tom of rolling green hills, leprechauns and shamrocks. As he collected his scattered thoughts and began to fill in Flannigan on their progress, it became clearer to Tom that what had begun as a promising investigation had degraded into a waiting game. Tom recounted what he knew to John. Travaglia and two other unknown men had sped through Apollo in a 1977 silver blue Lancia and goaded Leonard Miller into chasing them. After Leonard stopped them, one of the men in the car shot Leonard twice with a .38-caliber revolver.

Both men agreed that it was comforting to know that Leonard had gotten off six shots. Tom attributed it to good training, and John agreed. Both men knew that tiny victories amid such a catastrophic event were all that they could hope for, and each secretly vowed to hold onto those tiny victories for all they were worth.

Leonard's killers had escaped along Route 66 and then abandoned the Lancia near Holiday Park, where they hitched a ride into McKeesport. Although he hadn't been able to confirm it, Tom was pretty sure that the Lancia was stolen. All of these things Tom knew, and now so did John Flannigan. What neither man knew, but which both desperately wanted to know, was the answer to the question, where was Michael Travaglia?

Tom reminded Flannigan about Chuck Lutz's Sonny's Lounge warrant, Daniel Keith and Ray Scalese (both of whom he hoped were with Michael) and thanked him in advance for anything that he and his men might be able to do.

Tom Tridico heard the vacant hum of the dial tone in his ear before he even realized that his conversation was over. Numb and bone weary, he lowered the phone into its cradle and stared at the blank desk blotter on the desk in front of him. Tom was not a man who easily admitted defeat. Inside, that voice that always haunted him when he hit a brick wall in a case began to nag at him. Warning him that if they didn't pick up the trail of the killers soon, it would grow stale, the voice reminded him of how impotent he was—how human. Tom knew that when the trail goes cold, the odds of solving a case drop drastically. In Tom's world, failure was never an option, and the few times when it did happen, he took the defeat to heart. Victims left unspoken for, deaths unaccounted for and killer's unpunished all swirled in Tom's mind—a seething, jumbled mess.

Slowly, the face of Leonard Miller crept into the swirling stew of his past and stared at Tom. Expressionless and blank, Leonard's face looked just as it had twelve hours earlier at the roadside as Tom kneeled over his body—when Tom had made his promise.

Kneeling beside Leonard Miller, Tom had promised him secretly, silently and earnestly that he would find the killers. He promised Leonard that he would speak for him and would stand up for him to make sure that his blood was not spilled in vain. As Tom Tridico sat in that station house, at that desk, alone with Leonard Miller, he slowly began to realize that he might not be able to keep his promise. For the first time in his thirty-year career, Tom Tridico was scared.

Part IV

The Search Is On

John Flannigan spread his notebook out on the podium and looked out over his detectives. He shuffled several papers. His men stared at him in silent anticipation. News such as the murder of a fellow officer spreads like wildfire through the police community, so Flannigan's men were already fully aware that Tom Tridico and his men were tracking a cop killer. They all knew why they were there. What they didn't know, and what Flannigan was about to tell them, was that they were going to be crucial in solving the case.

Flannigan began in even, unemotional, measured tones, in his characteristic low-key, almost ambivalent delivery. He offered his men the tiny scraps of information that most already knew anyway. The men stirred, restlessly. They were men of action. Sitting in briefings and talking about solutions were not options these men tolerated well. Frank Amity spoke up first.

"Look, Sarge, I know this Scalese guy. How about me and Tony go scarf this prick up and see what he knows?"

Flannigan shared his men's enthusiasm and action-oriented outlook on police work, but the stripes that often sat heavy on his shoulders forced him to tighten the reigns a little from time to time.

"Look, we're gonna head out momentarily. Let's just not go off half-cocked." Respect for Flannigan was universal among his men, and they stirred but held their seats for a moment longer. "PSP thinks this guy Travaglia might also be running with a kid name Daniel K. Montgomery."

Condemi piped up, "We got pictures on any of these mopes?"

"Tridico sent me a photo of Michael Travaglia, but the other two skells, we've got nothing on." Flannigan continued, "Montgomery may hang out downtown, and according to what PSP knows, he's got a real distinct West Virginia accent. They said you can't miss it." Flannigan hesitated. "Might be these guys hang out downtown, near Liberty and Ninth."

"Gay Avenue?" asked Condemi.

"Yeah. Travaglia's suspected in the murder of this guy Levato. PSP's intel points to Levato being gay. They think maybe he was trollin' downtown and got picked up by the wrong guys."

Condemi nodded.

"We're also looking for a church organist from the south side named William Nicholls."

"He a suspect, too?" Amity asked.

"No. Might be another victim though. Again, PSP's working under the assumption he's same deal as Levato. If that's the case, they were all probably hanging out down around the Edison looking for some action."

"Sounds like they got more action than they were bargaining for," Tom Condemi quipped.

Flannigan pretended that he didn't hear the remark.

"Where do you want us to start looking, Sarge?" Tom Liberti asked, breaking the tension.

"Me and Tony are headed over to Twenty-first on the south side. This Scalese guy owes me one anyway," Amity interrupted.

Flannigan glanced at Tony. "Okay. You two find Scalese. Rest of you guys fan out downtown. Hit your local spots, roust your CI's and rattle every goddamn cage in the city till these murderous pukes crawl out from under their rock. Remember, these guy's are cop killers. Wait for backup and no bullshit heroics. I mean it."

Before he had even flipped the cover closed on his notebook, Flannigan's men were already out the door. Eager to get a few minutes alone with Michael Travaglia, each man left the briefing gunning for a confrontation.

Tom Tridico paced around the confines of his tiny office. At times like this the small space felt even more claustrophobic than normal. It had been an hour since any of his men had checked in. He had spoken with John Flannigan, but he didn't have any news either. His men were saturating the city, hoping to flush out Michael Travaglia. Until they did, Tom was in wait-and-see mode. Four years in the navy and thirty years as a cop doesn't prepare you for "wait and see." They prepare you for "go and do," which is just what Tom wanted. The problem was that right now, there was nothing for Tom to go and do, so he waited—and paced.

He reviewed his notes, worked on his report and began calling all the troopers whom he had out in the field. One by one, he checked with them all. Dickey and Boyerinas were getting nowhere. Likewise with Lutz and Luniewski. There wasn't much more to report from any of the others, either. Tom's men had been on duty since well before sunup. Under normal circumstances, the overtime that these men were working would have to be officially authorized. These weren't normal circumstances. Administrative bullshit, Tom thought, could simply take a backseat to operational effectiveness.

Every time Tom sat down, Leonard Miller reminded him how much farther and farther away Michael Travaglia was getting. Tom began to wonder whether Travaglia was even in the state anymore. If I'd killed a cop, he thought, I sure as hell wouldn't stick around. Then of course, he thought of the irony of this and brushed it aside, knowing full well that he did not think like a criminal, nor did this criminal think like a cop. He decided to assume that Travaglia had not gotten far and would show himself again.

Tom leaned back in his chair. It was an uncomfortable, fifteen-year-old wooden chair. He'd brought it with him when he transferred to the Greensburg barracks, but every time he sat in it he swore he'd throw it out the next day. Uncomfortable or no, as Tom leaned against the back of the wooden chair, his eyes drifted closed. Eventually, the tumultuous thoughts and fears began to recede. Finally, even the cold blank stare of Leonard Miller left his aching brain, and he began to drift into a fitful but deep sleep.

Frank Amity weaved his way through the light, post–rush hour traffic and made his way to Brady Street. Making the right onto Brady, he waited for an opening, merged onto Forbes Avenue and headed for the Birmingham Bridge. Connecting the Oakland neighborhoods surrounding the University of Pittsburgh with the south side, Birmingham Bridge empties onto Carson Street, and Frank hung a quick right heading west onto Carson.

Having dealt with him in the past, Amity knew that Ray Scalese was a lowlife. A perennial pain in Amity's ass, Scalese was a local street thug with so little ambition that he barely made for a passable criminal. Frank figured that homicide was a pretty big step up for him. Covering the one and a half blocks to Twenty-first Street quickly, Frank made a left and headed out toward Mission Street and South Side Park. As he passed the dilapidated, dingy apartments that crammed the roadside, Frank kept his eyes peeled for Ray. He knew that Ray was hardly able to keep a job, so he figured it was likely that he was on foot.

Within a minute or two, Frank was pulling the unmarked city police car alongside the curb in front of Ray's apartment building.

"Look, this skell is probably harmless, but if he's wrapped up in this cop killing, there's no sense in taking any chances." He paused. Condemi stared at him as if to say, "And?"

"Let's just be careful." Frank Amity could not believe that he had said something so cheesy.

The door to Ray's place was no different from the rest. Amity was working from memory, but he was sure that they were standing in front of the right door. Frank had his hand on his gun. He wanted to play this low key, so he figured that kicking in the door with guns out and throwing Ray around would be a bit over-the-top. He decided to try the subtle approach.

Amity rapped hard on the door in that unmistakable police knock that is practically standard academy issue. He heard stirring inside the apartment. Footsteps grew louder on the other side of the door and then stopped. He could feel eyes straining through the peephole. Frank imagined that he heard heavy breathing through the door.

A woman's voice called out, "Who's there?"

Frank looked at Tony. Tony's contorted, puzzled look said it all.

"Police. Open the door," Frank announced.

"Show me a badge," the faceless voice retorted.

Frank fished inside his jacket pocket, pulled out his shield and flashed it in front of the peephole. Moments later, the rattle and clack of the safety chain clattered against the door and the deadbolt clicked. A second later, the door cracked open an inch and a middle-aged woman squished her face into the opening.

"What do you want?"

"I'm Frank Amity, Pittsburgh Police. I'm looking for Ray."

"Ray Scalese?"

"Yes ma'am. He home?"

"Ray don't live here no more. I'm his landlady. I kicked him out a couple days ago."

Frank shot a dejected look to his partner. "You know where he went?"

"No. You might check out Doggone Sam's. He works there, I think."

"Downtown?" Frank confirmed.

"Yeah, Ninth and Penn."

"Thanks."

The door began to swing closed, stopped and flew wide open. "You see that bum, you tell Ray he owes me back rent," she ordered.

"Yes ma'am, we'll do." Frank chuckled as he and Tony Condemi crept back through the hallways of Ray Scalese's former home. When the two men reached the car, Tony turned to Frank and winked, "Feel like a hot dog?"

Frank Amity and Tony Condemi piled into their unmarked car and headed out of the south side and back into the city, still in search of Ray Scalese.

DOGGONE SAM'S

On the ride back across Birmingham Bridge, Frank radioed Flannigan. It was a long shot, but Frank figured that he'd better check out Doggone Sam's just in case Ray was still holding down a job there. Without much detail, Frank let Flannigan know that he needed some backup to meet him around the corner from Ninth and Penn Avenues. Amity would fill them in when they got there.

Emerging from the north end of the bridge, Amity caught the light onto Fifth Avenue and made the left heading past Moultrie Street and Meyers Plumbing Supply. Fifth Avenue was a straight shot downtown to Grant Street and took forever during rush hour. With fifteen traffic lights in as many city blocks, timing was everything. Lucky for Amity and Condemi, traffic signals are optional when you're a city detective on the trail of a cop killer. The twenty-minute drive took Frank a little over seven. When Frank hit Grant Street, he began crisscrossing across the heart of the city toward Penn Avenue. He zipped up Smithfield to Liberty and made a left onto Tenth. Killing his headlights, he flew down Exchange Way, barely missing the fire hydrant on the corner. Halfway down the alleyway, he pulled in behind a rancid Dempster dumpster and waited.

Tony Condemi looked at the more senior detective with a queasy, "Who the hell taught you to drive?" look.

"What?" Frank scoffed.

"You are one non-driving individual, Frank."

Amity snorted and pushed his door open, banging it off the dumpster.

By the time Frank and Tony had closed the car doors, a second blacked-out, unmarked unit was rolling down the alley. Regis Liberi, Ron Freeman and John Leckei piled out of the dirt-encrusted police car and joined Frank and Tony. Frank briefed the other three members of the squad and gave them each perimeter assignments. Frank didn't think that Ray would make a run for it, but then again, he hadn't thought that Ray would be involved in a cop killing either.

Exchange Way dead ended on Ninth Street about one hundred yards south from the corner of Ninth and Penn. The five plainclothes detectives emerged from its shadow with a forced casualness that immediately telegraphed both their occupation and their mission. Nonetheless, with most people driven indoors by the frigid night, they walked the short block and a half to Doggone Sam's unnoticed.

Amity stationed Liberi, Freeman and Leckei outside in case Ray bolted and then took Condemi inside with him. The perennial smell of stale hot dogs, onions and Pine-Sol still filled the tiny, cramped restaurant. Frank didn't want a hot dog after all. Behind the counter, the old man was swabbing the floors with a one-hundred-year-old mop, and a young man in a heavy parka nursed a soda at a table near the door. Amity recognized the older man. He studied the soda-sipping boy. It was not Ray. He decided that the boy was not an immediate concern and continued walking.

Without missing a stroke of mopping, the old man nodded to Amity and Condemi as they walked up.

"I'm looking for Ray Scalese. He work here?"

"Yeah. He works here, but he ain't in tonight. He'll be here tomorrow," said the old man as he jammed the frayed strands of mop into a crevice under the counter. It was another dead end. The two detectives turned to leave—empty-handed.

"Ray lives around the corner on Liberty Avenue," the man in the parka said in a thick West Virginia accent.

Immediately, Amity halted in mid-stride. Condemi looked at Amity and then stepped between the seated man and the door. Amity approached him and asked him for identification. Cautiously, the man reached into his pocket, pulled out a brown leather wallet and flipped it open. As he handed Amity a tattered West Virginia driver's license, the hairs on Condemi's neck began to bristle.

Amity covertly signaled to Condemi with a gentle nod of the head and then took Daniel K. Montgomery by the arm.

"Let's step outside for a minute."

The three men stepped through the door onto Liberty Avenue. Liberi, Freeman and Leckei quickly joined them. They placed Montgomery up against the frozen brick building, and Amity pressed the point of his knee into the inside of Montgomery's leg to keep him off balance. He searched him. Patting down the outside of his jacket, Amity paused when he reached the right pocket. He carefully pushed his hand into the pocket and then withdrew a silver .38-caliber revolver with a two-inch barrel. Amity handed the gun to Condemi, who flipped the cylinder open, showed Frank the six stuffed chambers and then snapped it closed, palmed it and stuffed it into his jacket for safekeeping.

Resuming the search with greater enthusiasm, Amity probed every inch of Montgomery's clothing. When he was done, he added twenty unspent .38-caliber bullets to the handgun that his partner was now holding.

"Danny, you're under arrest for possession of an illegal firearm."

Daniel Montgomery began stammering and stuttering in his thick Appalachian mountaineer dialect. Daniel swore on everything he could think of that the gun wasn't his.

"Listen, you gotta believe me. I'm just holding the gun for a guy."

"Oh yeah. I've heard it all be before, Danny," Condemi said.

"No. Really. The guy's name is Michael Travaglia."

Five sets of eyes drilled into Daniel Montgomery as time seemed to stand still. Amity spoke first. "How do you know Michael Travaglia?"

"He came in here about an hour ago. He wanted me to go with him and John over to their room at the Edison. When we got there, he handed me the gun and the bullets."

"Go on," Amity said.

"He told me to hold 'em for him. He said he killed a cop with it and he needed to get rid of it for a while." Montgomery pleaded with his eyes for the detectives to believe him.

Amity studied Daniel for a moment. "All the same, you're coming with us," he said as he pulled Montgomery's arms behind him and slipped handcuffs on the mountaineer. The six men disappeared down Exchange Way.

When the group of detectives arrived in the alley behind the Edison Hotel, Daniel Montgomery was seated, handcuffed, in the backseat of Frank Amity's car next to Tony Condemi. Condemi had the disappointing task of babysitting Montgomery, while the remaining four detectives checked out his story at the Edison Hotel. As the men assembled in the tiny parking lot at the corner of Garrison Place and French Street, close enough to see the Edison but not be seen by its occupants, they quickly gave their equipment a once over and then let Frank Amity know that they were ready.

At 9:45 p.m., Amity and his squad entered the lobby of the hotel. Seated behind the shabby counter was Albert Bortz, the night manager. Amity flashed his shield to the unimpressed innkeeper.

"Who's in room 616?" he asked.

The innkeeper nonchalantly slid the guest register out from under the desk, thumbed through it and paused.

"You need a warrant or something?" he asked.

"No. Who's in room 616?"

He eyed the detectives skeptically. Hopelessly outnumbered, Bortz flipped to the page and read off the names. "Michael Simmons and John Lesko."

Simmons was an alias for Travaglia, he thought. He nodded to his team. "We need to get into that room. You have a pass key?"

"Sure. You're sure you don't need a warrant?"

"I'm sure."

The manager grabbed a thick, jangly ring crammed full of keys and headed for the elevator in the middle of the lobby.

"Let's take the stairs," Frank said to him, and Bortz veered off course and headed toward the stairwell.

The five officers, guns drawn, crept up the stairs behind Albert Bortz as he wound his way up six flights. Frank Amity lead the way as, step after step, they inched closer and closer to a confrontation with two men they knew were capable of killing a police officer and were likely to choose a hail of gunfire over a quiet surrender.

When they reached the top of the stairs, Amity turned to his men and quickly checked them. Once he was sure that the other detectives were set, he motioned for the manager to open room 616. Albert Bortz stepped up to the door and quietly slid the key into the lock. Gently turning it, he stepped back and nodded to Frank Amity.

TRAVAGLIA AND LESKO ARE APPREHENDED

Night had fallen on quiet Apollo, Pennsylvania. The darkness of the January sky that blanketed the valley seemed a bit thicker and more oppressive to the men and women who had gathered at the tiny little police station on Pennsylvania Avenue.

Every inch of the station held reminders of Leonard Miller. Chief Rick Murphy, Officers Robin Davis, Jim Clawson, Jack Gibbons, Mark Fetterman and a handful of others who knew Leonard Miller as a close personal friend had come together to mourn the loss of a gentle soul and heroic man.

Apollo mayor William Kerr, as stunned and grief-stricken as the officers, met with them to share his condolences, as well as to offer the encouraging news that the state police felt confident that they were closing in on Leonard's assailants. The sincere words offered little comfort in the chilling Apollo squad room filled with long, drawn faces and puffy eyelids.

Stoic under the toughest conditions, these officers took no shame in the tears that crept down their faces, barely offering to conceal them. Words filtered around the room, fleeting smiles came and went and Leonard's legacy was shared among his colleagues. The long process of healing in this warrior's world was beginning. The rituals of death that so permeate police culture and are so necessary for closure had begun.

These officers knew that in three short days, hundreds of uniformed men and women would line the streets of this town and join them to honor one of their own. Outsiders would stand by and watch with awe and respect as the seemingly endless line of police cars snaked its way behind the sleek black hearse up Second Street and out to First Lutheran Church, wondering and trying to understand.

The honor guard, with military precision and tear-stained, grey granite faces, would escort Leonard past his parents and into the church and stand guard among the throng of mourners hoping to say one last goodbye to the man whom they wished they had known better—or at all.

Thousands would file past the flag-draped coffin carrying Leonard home, solemnly and hopefully praying for a peaceful rest for the man whose life was taken in utter hatred and violence so soon before his time and so senselessly.

In three days, this would all come to pass. Nevertheless, for now, the ritual shared among these few, the ones for whom Leonard's death meant more than most, would be a private affair—closed to outsiders. At this moment in time, the ultimate show of solidarity, the thread that runs deep among all police officers and across all generations, pulled these men and women together for one last time to speak in soft, wavering voices; to speak the words of comfort that attempt to make sense of a senseless act.

Mortal men can scarcely comprehend a death that touched so many, and yet, it is mortal men whom we expect to bring sense out of it. With Leonard's passing, the fleeting and fragile flame of compassion wavered in the night and, for a moment, was snuffed out. But, as with hope, compassion is an eternal flame borne by the men and women who honor him, and it sparked anew here in the somber little station house fifty miles from where Michael Travaglia and John Lesko awaited the rush of police detectives. For as Leonard touched so many, he passed on that flame with the confident knowledge that no sacrifice, great or small, could forever extinguish it. Leonard served with honor, with pride and with dignity; and in his death, these men and women grieved. Yet in his honor, they would carry on the flame of compassion and service that he so clearly sparked.

As the quiet collection of officers filed from the station, the process of healing and understanding was still years from complete. However, in those moments of shared private communion, the reality of man's mortality and the fragility of life had been pushed a little bit farther toward the backs of their minds. The communal grief shared by these brothers in arms would allow them to lay their heads on their pillows, rise again in the daylight and once more feel the tug of forty pounds of leather, steel and lead against their hips. They would move forward and carry on the honorable calling that they had shared with Leonard—their hearts would be heavier, but they would carry on.

The door to room 616 flew open, rebounded off the wall and clattered back into Frank Amity as he stormed into the room. A thunderous chorus of police commands and shouted orders exploded in the air as the remaining four men ran headlong behind him into the room.

Michael Travaglia was dressed in jeans and a torn sweatshirt, and a look of utter shock flashed onto his face. Staring at the men, his eyes leapt first to one, then to another and then to the doorway. He leapt to his feet and sprang toward the open door. The room was polluted with police officers.

As he sprinted for the door, a detective took a step to his left and cut off his escape route. With no path to freedom, two detectives pounced on him and immediately wrestled him to the ground. A grunt escaped his lips as his body fell beneath the weight of two burly detectives. With one on each arm, they forced his flailing hands behind his back and snapped first one and then the other handcuff onto him.

On the other side of the tiny room, Frank Amity had cornered John Lesko. He stood motionless beside the bed. His face was blank, emotionless, and he stared into Amity's eyes without actually seeing. In a flash, John reached beneath the sheet and seized the .22-caliber revolver hidden there. As Lesko raised the revolver toward Amity, Frank began screaming for him to drop the gun. As John Lesko's arm raised higher and higher, Frank Amity's right index finger pulled tighter and tighter. When Frank had about six pounds of trigger pull on the seven-pound trigger, John Lesko's face registered an epiphany. Apparently sensing immediate death and choosing to live to fight another day, John relaxed his grip on the gun and let the revolver slip from his grasp. As the .22 clattered to the floor, Frank wondered if John Lesko knew just how close he had come to being on the business end of a .357-caliber bullet.

Once the revolver hit the floor, Amity and the two remaining detectives leaped onto Lesko and wrestled him to the carpet. Without resistance, John slipped to the ground and placed his arms behind his back. The *clack-clack* of a pair of Smith & Wesson handcuffs was music to Frank Amity and his partners' ears. It signaled the end of a tortuous manhunt.

John Lesko and Michael Travaglia were in custody. After a weeklong rampage spanning three counties, police had apprehended them without exchanging a single shot. Frank Amity, Tony Condemi, Regis Liberi, Ronald Freeman, John Leckei and the other men of Pittsburgh's homicide bureau had been victorious.

Police led the two men down from room 616 and through the lobby where they had so recently targeted and kidnapped their victims. As they walked from the hotel to the waiting police cruisers, there was a sigh of relief that escaped along the valley and up the three rivers. The police had finely arrested these murderous, violent men. The system upon which we all rely to keep society safe had succeeded, and justice would force these barbarous monsters to take responsibility for the heinous acts they had committed.

As the ebullient officers exchanged handshakes and high-fives, the two damaged men disappeared down Penn Avenue in a cloud of exhaust and gently dancing snowflakes. Now en route to Western Avenue's police headquarters, Michael Travaglia and John Lesko's reign of terror was over.

Friday, January 4, 1980, 2:00 a.m.

Tom Tridico jerked awake to the sound of his desk phone nearly clattering off its cradle. Groggy, he leaned forward in his creaky, fifteen-year-old wooden chair and rubbed the sleep from his eyes. On the seventh ring, Tom finally reached over and snatched up the receiver, silencing the incessant ruckus.

"Tridico."

Still wrapped in sleep's twilight, Tom stared blankly ahead as he listened to the caller on the other end.

"I see. I see. That's great. Fantastic job. I'm on my way."

Tom slowly lowered the receiver onto its cradle and sat staring straight ahead. Then he glanced at his watch. He smiled. Less than twenty-four hours after Leonard Miller's body fell to the cold pavement outside Apollo, the men who had snatched his young life away from him were in custody. Tom knew that he had a great deal of work left to do, but the suspects were talking, and he knew that confessions always make for stronger cases. He was optimistic.

Tom stood and stretched his aching legs, and as he prepared to head to the Pittsburgh Police Department, he thought about justice, good and evil and promises—and he was relieved. Tom Tridico was no longer scared.

Epilogue

On the day of Leonard Miller's funeral, mourners arrived in the tiny town of Apollo by the hundreds, some from as far away as Johnstown near the center of the state. Most knew Leonard only by the photo that had appeared in the *Valley News Dispatch* just days before, yet all of them drove the hundred or so miles necessary to pay their respects to a comrade. As the church filled with solemn-faced police officers, one could not help but be taken aback by the Christmas decorations that still adorned the altar.

Leonard Miller's death had followed behind one of the most holy Christian holidays, so closely in fact that many could not help but note the significance of this throng of congregants gathering to pay respects to a man who had sacrificed his life so that others may have safety.

Evelyn and Frank Miller sat in the front of the church—silently, with dignity, with pride—as Chief Rick Murphy and Officers Thomas Coulter, Jim Clawson, Robin Davis and Donny Mahan slowly escorted the flag-draped coffin of the fallen officer into the church. The somber silence inside the First Lutheran Church rippled with soft sobs as Leonard's pallbearers carried his casket past the seven hundred mourners and down the aisle toward the altar.

The angelic strains of "Oh Touch Me Lord" filtered through the air as Reverend Frederick Zikeli took his place in the pulpit and prepared to address the gathering. Speaking in solemn and reverent tones, he called upon the parishioners to honor Leonard for his high and noble goals, lest they be in vain. "We have lost a good friend, a committed citizen, a fellow police officer," he continued, urging the throng of mourners not to forget the wonderful soul and person Leonard Miller was.

The scriptural quote printed on the front of the bulletin, "There is no greater love than this, that a man should lay down his life for his friends," seemed to capture the enduring spirit that began to fill the church as remembrances of Leonard Miller echoed through it, honoring who he was and what he had meant to so many people.

As Mayor Bill Kerr, struggling with the overwhelming emotion of the moment, approached Frank and Evelyn Miller, silence overwhelmed the congregation. When he presented the Millers with a posthumous commendation for Leonard's heroic service, he offered, "For what he said, for what he did, for what he stood for, Leonard will always be at our side."

As Leonard's pallbearers carried his coffin from the church, the gentle rustle of fabric broke the still, frozen silence as the eighty uniformed officers in Leonard's Honor Guard snapped to attention and, with military precision, offered one final salute. Those who could, held back their tears. Those who could not, wept as the young officer's body was gently slipped into the hearse and began its final ascent up First Street toward the cemetery.

The crisp report of the twenty-one-gun salute and the final strains of the bugler's horn have long since faded from the hills above the Kiskiminetas River where Leonard Miller's body lies. The scars left by his passing have not. For the people Leonard touched, there is no amount of time, no measure of justice and no explanation that will ever fully close those wounds. They are destined to remain close to the surface.

He was a man of honor. He was a man of justice, and above all, he was a man of heart. His passion and compassion have become legendary, and to this day local residents honor and remember him. From the Leonard Miller Adelphoi House for troubled youth to the Leonard Miller Memorial Bridge that now stands where he lost his life, his friends have not forgotten. Determined that Leonard's high and noble goals, his sense of pride in public service and his commitment to selfless sacrifice will not be forgotten, fellow officers such as Robin Davis, Jim Clawson and the many others who have followed in his footsteps carry on his tradition of service.

In Bill Kerr's own heartfelt condolences to the Millers, he summarized the truth underlying the pain and hurt: "Leonard will always be at our side."

And so it was his presence that I felt nearly thirty years ago as I walked down the dimly lit hallway leading from the station house out onto Pennsylvania Avenue. And following in his silent footsteps, I rattled the doors of the plaza and carried on his legacy and his promise just as thousands of other officers have done. Leonard's true legacy, and that for which we shall always remember him, is that which truly identified him as a giant among men—he understood that "there is no greater love than this, that a man should lay down his life for his friends." For that, we are all truly grateful.

Afterword

In homicide investigation, statistics bear out the adage that you are three times more likely to die at the hands of an acquaintance than at those of a stranger. While random acts of violence are certainly known to occur, it is the domestic squabble or the drunken bar fight that is more likely to snuff out your life.

In the puzzling world of Michael Travaglia and John Lesko, these normal precursors to murder are practically nonexistent. The randomness—the inability of either man to point to a single identifiable "why"—has shocked and perplexed the men who investigated the aftermath of Travaglia and Lesko's ruthless binge. Indeed, it is this very question that the news media and the family and friends of four innocent people continue to ask to this day.

As often happens, in the days and weeks following things of this nature, rampant speculation gained momentum, fueled by bits and fragments of the truth as it filtered down to the public. Among them, most frequently discussed were the obvious drug, alcohol and satanic involvements that the men themselves had identified as possible precipitating events. However, the reality, which makes the weeklong episode that much more bewildering, is that, even thirty years later, neither man can definitively explain what within him snapped, sending him careening down the slope of psychopathic murder and blood lust.

By the time the story had been told and all the facts were recorded in detailed taped statements, the better part of January 4 had slipped away.

Michael Steffee and Tom Tridico had recovered William Nicholls's body, and the Pittsburgh Police Department could take pride in a job well done. By taking the pair into custody, they had put an end to a chain of events that reached far beyond the boundaries of their city.

What had begun eight days earlier had traversed three counties and reached as far away as sixty miles. It had touched the lives of dozens of family and friends and involved nearly one hundred officers in an unprecedented manhunt. It had ensnared four unsuspecting, unaware victims in a trap of mortal danger. When it ended, the Pennsylvania State Police and the Pittsburgh Police had fulfilled their promise to society and to their community and had tracked the killers to a successful conclusion.

Law enforcement had done its job. From there, the court system took over and began the next phase of the criminal justice process. This phase has dragged on for thirty years.

Appendix

In the Travaglia and Lesko cases, prosecutors had to make a multitude of complex decisions quickly, and each would affect the outcome of the case dramatically. Exactly what to charge the defendants with, whether to hold separate or consolidated trials, which cases to prosecute first and other equally difficult strategic and legal questions would color the final verdict of each defendant's case. The men charged with making these decisions were Gregory Olson and Albert Nichols, district attorneys for Indiana and Westmoreland Counties, respectively.

Olson and Nichols made the decision to offer the defendants a deal in Indiana County and try them for Leonard Miller's murder in Westmoreland County. As part of this plea, Olson agreed to defer sentencing of both defendants on the Nicholls murder until after the trial of Officer Miller. This was a decision that would have far-reaching implications.

Lesko and Travaglia both agreed to this arrangement, and on May 19, 1980, in front of Judge Robert C. Earley, both pleaded guilty to second-degree murder in Indiana County. Although they would later file a motion to withdraw their pleas and stand trial for the Nicholls murder, the judge would deny that motion.

Having effectively disposed of the three companion cases in Indiana County, prosecutors were now free to focus entirely on prosecuting Lesko and Travaglia for Leonard Miller's murder. As part of their strategy, prosecutors decided to offer fifteen-year-old Ricky Rutherford a grant of immunity from prosecution for the murder of Miller in return for his testimony implicating the remaining two defendants in the homicide.

Any time a prosecutor agrees to trade charges for testimony, there are far-reaching implications. These implications include the credibility of the witness, as well as the ethicality of offering an admitted killer what amounts to a free pass for murder. However, whether the state would have been successful in convicting Travaglia and Lesko without the testimony of Rutherford is questionable.

What the prosecutors lacked, and what the confessions of both men failed to establish in these cases, was intent. To remedy this, prosecutors were confronted with the unenviable choice of exchanging Ricky Rutherford's testimony regarding the intent of the other two defendants for his freedom. Without it, prosecutors already knew that Travaglia and Lesko would possibly be able to avoid a conviction for first-degree murder, maybe sidestep second-degree murder and could even end up with a conviction for felony murder. This meant the difference between the death penalty and perhaps ten to fifteen years in prison—maximum. Faced with this dilemma, Nichols chose the lesser of the two evils and struck a deal with Rutherford for his testimony.

With the crucial components of the case in place, the prosecution was set to move forward. After the court heard and disposed of a number of standard—and some creative—pretrial motions, the defendants were set for a joint trial early in January 1981. On January 5, 1981, jury selection began, and on January 19, a fully qualified jury was empanelled. The trial got underway the week of January 21.

The standard litany of witnesses paraded before the jury, including Tridico, his team, ballistic and laboratory experts and, as expected, Ricky Rutherford. Rutherford's testimony about the killing of William Nicholls—over defense objection—and the facts leading up to the shooting of Leonard Miller were crucial to the prosecution's case.

Rutherford's testimony was everything that Albert Nichols had hoped for. Between his description of the killing of Nicholls and his statement detailing Lesko's warning—"Lay down in the back. This is gonna turn into a shooting gallery"—Rutherford proved to be worth his cost to the prosecutor. Establishing that Travaglia had the intent to kill and that Miller was not just the victim of an accidental shooting was in Rutherford's hands, and the prosecution's confidence seemed well placed.

While neither defendant took the stand, the prosecution introduced and read transcripts of their taped confessions for the jury. For prosecutors, allowing the jury to hear the defendant's own words is a valuable tool. The emotional impact it can have on the jury is beyond question.

Undoubtedly, the totality of the evidence that the prosecution paraded before the jury was quite convincing because on January 30, 1981, the jury convicted both John Lesko and Michael Travaglia of first-degree murder and conspiracy to commit murder. It was a victory for the prosecution, but celebration would have to wait until the conclusion of the penalty phase of the trial.

During the penalty phase of the trial, the prosecutor argued for the death penalty based on both Leonard Miller's status as an on-duty police officer and the previous guilty plea entered for William Nicholls's murder in Indiana County. To counter this, the defense called a number of character witnesses to establish John Lesko's and Michael Travaglia's disadvantaged childhoods in an attempt to mitigate against the death penalty.

At the conclusion of the evidence, the jury determined that the aggravating circumstances outweighed the mitigating circumstances, and it sentenced both defendants to death. After the court denied several post-trial motions, the Court of Common Pleas for Westmoreland County, Pennsylvania, formally sentenced John Lesko and Michael Travaglia to death in Pennsylvania's electric chair.

The long and strenuous process of prosecuting a death penalty case was finally over. Albert Nichols could now rest soundly, knowing that he had mounted and won an overwhelmingly successful prosecution of two undisputedly evil men. The verdict was in. The judge had excused the jury and had imposed the final adjudication of guilty and a formal sentence. It was time for celebration. Unfortunately, that celebration would be very short-lived.

When confronted with such undoubtedly deserving defendants, the often squeaky wheels of justice become most noticeable in the appellate process. While our ancestors founded our country on the notion of due process and fairness, the actual workings of the cogs and gears that constitute due process are often quite unsightly. The average layperson views the possibility of a court overturning a conviction on a technicality as a failing of the system. It is not a failing. It is unfortunate; it is not, however, a failing.

As unsightly as the results in a single case may be, they are necessary in the larger picture to ensure that we accord everyone a fair trial and that the results of the trial process are accurate. The revered legal scholar William Blackstone once said, "Better that ten guilty persons escape, than that one innocent suffer." Known as the Blackstone ratio, this ten-to-one ratio has come to symbolize the classic western view about the tradeoff between efficiency and accuracy.

Not surprisingly, this notion of justice and fairness is not without its detractors. Jeremy Bentham, enlightenment philosopher, Utilitarian and originator of the "hedonistic calculus," a premise that underlies our justifications for punishment, views the Blackstone ratio somewhat more skeptically.

Bentham warned that this notion of withholding punishment from the guilty for fear of wrongly imprisoning the innocent was a slippery slope that ran the risk of immunizing criminal conduct for a lack of absolute certainty in the outcome of the process. He urged that we "guard against those sentimental exaggerations which tend to give crime impunity, under the pretext of insuring the safety of innocence." Whether Bentham or Blackstone held the more reasoned view is still up for debate. However, regardless of the side of the fence you land on, cases such as the Michael Travaglia and John Lesko ordeal point out the far extremes of our system.

This case illustrates well that for every Clarence Earl Gideon or Ernesto Miranda, whose historical cases offer clear-cut examples of systemic failures in gross need of correction, there are a Lesko and Travaglia out there for whom thirty years of appeals tend to call into question the very validity of the system such safeguards are intended to protect.

While Lesko and Travaglia are not the oldest members of America's death row, they are definitely among the more senior. Having spent twenty-eight years filing appeals, winning new trials and ultimately winding up back on death row, only to win more appeals, their example has come to symbolize the essence of what both sides of this debate symbolize.

In purely evidentiary terms, neither of these men has denied that they committed the acts of which they are accused. The evidence of their guilt appears practically incontrovertible. Instead, this case has become one of the quintessential battles of technical rules. What's more, the added significance of the controversy surrounding the death penalty creates a literal life-or-death struggle that plays out through the legal shuffling of papers.

Pro-abolition advocates point to John Lesko as an archetypal exemplar of the principle that mentally deficient defendant's should not be executed. They cite examples of his abhorrent childhood and the abuse and deprivation he suffered at the hands of his mother and grandmother and argue that his upbringing resulted in a mind damaged so far beyond comprehension that to punish him with death would be both inhuman and outside the bounds of our notions of justice and fair play.

In the other camp, pro-reform and pro–death penalty adherents point to the unquestionable guilt and indisputable depravity of their acts as evidence that death is both a fitting and logical punishment for such depraved human beings. As Tom Tridico once said, "This is a classic case that deserves no second guessing as to whether the death penalty is justified." Perhaps it is the very fact that both of these men have confessed completely to their crimes that gives an odd sort of righteousness to this side of the debate. On the other hand, both our Supreme Court and many respected legal scholars agree that putting severely mentally disabled people to death is unconscionable under the Constitution.

Regardless of which faction you align with, the fact remains that this is the backdrop onto which the appeals process was cast twenty-eight years ago. Attorneys for both defendants have waged appeal after appeal, beginning with standard post-trial motions and continuing all the way to the Supreme Court of the United States.

Attorneys have used reams of paper to brief dozens of issues. On some issues, such as whether prosecutor Albert Nichols improperly asked the jury to exact vengeance for the killings of four innocent people by putting Lesko and Travaglia to death, the defendants have won. On most others, they have not.

Wending their way through the system, the defendants, through separate efforts, eventually exhausted their direct appeals options and each eventually succeeded in securing at least partial victories.

Having exhausted all state remedies and being largely unsuccessful, Lesko filed a habeas corpus petition with the United States District Court for the Western District of Pennsylvania, challenging the use of the Nicholls guilty plea during the sentencing phase of his trial, as well as challenging several comments by the prosecutor during his closing arguments.

After bouncing between the United States District Court and the United States Court of Appeals for the Third Circuit, the Third Circuit finally remanded Lesko's case to Westmoreland County for a retrial on the sentencing phase of the case, based on the prosecutor's improper closing argument.

In 1995, pursuant to the remand of the Third Circuit, Westmoreland County scheduled John Lesko for a resentencing hearing. During this hearing, Rabe Marsh III and Bryan O'Leary represented Lesko. In early February 1995, John Lesko's retrial began. After a full evidentiary hearing in front of a newly selected and empanelled jury, the jury once again sentenced John Lesko to death. Perhaps not surprisingly, this did not mark the end of the appellate process for Lesko.

Following numerous motions for post-conviction relief under Pennsylvania's PCRA (Post-Conviction Relief Act), a stay of execution and affirmance of Lesko's death sentence by the Pennsylvania State

Supreme Court, in 1999 Lesko's second trial counsel, Rabe Marsh III, withdrew as his attorney. His withdrawal would mark a drastic shift in the focus of the case.

With Marsh's withdrawal, Robert Brett Dunham of the Defender Association of Philadelphia, a nonprofit corporation dedicated to representing indigent defendants, took control of his case. Dunham, with a long-standing record of death penalty cases, took Lesko's case in a new direction.

Beginning in late 1999, Dunham began mounting an appeal on Lesko's behalf, arguing that his attorney during the second trial had failed to properly protect Lesko's interest. Raising a claim of ineffective assistance of counsel, Dunham began arguing that by failing to conduct a thorough investigation into John Lesko's horrific childhood, Marsh was unable to raise proper mitigating circumstances to counter the prosecution's aggravating circumstances.

In addition, Dunham's case calls into question Marsh's failure to challenge several key witnesses whom Dunham believed would have strongly disputed the prosecution's view of Lesko's mental state at the time of the killings.

Using these claims to propel the case forward, Dunham began his march through the court system. After numerous motions, delays, hearings and thousands of pages of legal memoranda, briefs and answers, Richard E. McCormick Jr., Westmoreland County judge, issued an order granting John Lesko not only a new sentencing trial, but also a new guilt-stage trial. On August 7, 2006, more than twenty-five years after being found guilty and sentenced to death, John Lesko was awarded not a second bite at the apple, but a third.

As one would expect, John Peck, the sitting district attorney for Westmoreland County, immediately filed a notice of appeal. In September 2006, this appeal, too, began winding its way through the Pennsylvania appellate courts. On December 1, 2008, the Commonwealth of Pennsylvania's appeal of John Lesko's overturned conviction and death sentence sits before the Pennsylvania Supreme Court, awaiting yet another decision in this labyrinthine, convoluted, thirty-year-old case.

While Michael Travaglia's case took a separate path throughout the appeals process, for the most part the story has been the same. Beginning with the nearly obligatory post-conviction trial court motions in a death penalty case, Dante Bertani, Westmoreland County's public defender, began pushing Travaglia's cause through the Pennsylvania court system. Eventually, in 1996, in part due to John Lesko's federal appeals court victory, Michael Travaglia was also granted a new sentencing trial.

Thus began a nine-year march toward a new trial for Michael Travaglia. As pretrial motions, legal jockeying for a better position and strategic preparation for the new courtroom showdown were underway, weeks, months and eventually years ticked away. After a trip to the Pennsylvania Supreme Court and an attempt at a federal habeas corpus petition, Judge John E. Blahovec was finally able to set a retrial date for Michael Travaglia's second shot at life.

On July 5, 2005, at 10:55 a.m., the voir dire of Michael Travaglia's retrial began. From this rigorous question-and-answer session, twelve of Michael's peers—nine women and three men—were selected. On July 13, at 11:13 a.m., the last of the panel had been selected and sworn, and trial number two for Michael Travaglia was finally underway—twenty-four years after a similarly charged jury of his peers had already sentenced him to die in Pennsylvania's electric chair.

On Friday, July 25, 2005, the ten-day ordeal began outright. Joined by assistant counsel Ned J. Nakles, Bertani's trial strategy differed somewhat from his colleague Rabe Marsh's strategy in the Lesko retrial. While Marsh focused primarily on Lesko's childhood misfortune, Bertani and Nakles directed the jury's attention to the evolution that Michael Travaglia had made during his time in prison. Taking the position that the forty-six-year-old Michael Travaglia who sat before the 2005 jury was a man who was truly different from the methamphetamine-crazed twenty-one-year-old originally convicted and sentenced to die in 1981, Bertani hoped to sway the jury to consider Michael's remarkable rehabilitation as mitigation to a sentence of death.

For the prosecution's part, John Peck—who had assumed control of the case from Albert Nichols when he left the district attorney's office—maintained a course very similar to his predecessor's in trying to achieve the same results.

Peck called many of the same witnesses, used much of the same line of attack and did a strong job of reminding the jurors of the horrors that Travaglia and Lesko had visited upon Leonard Miller and the three victims who preceded him in death.

Finally, on July 25, 2005, Judge Blahovec sent the case to the jury. With fewer than twenty-four hours of deliberation, the new jury in the Travaglia case returned with a verdict. The verdict? Death. Once again, the prosecution had successfully convinced twelve citizens of the merit of putting Michael Travaglia to death for the crimes he and his partner had committed in 1979. Not surprisingly, however, like John Lesko, this would not be the end of the story for Travaglia.

Even as deputies were leading Michael Travaglia away in handcuffs to the waiting sheriff's department transport unit for his ride back to death row, his attorneys were preparing the paperwork to start the appellate process anew.

A flurry of motions and briefs quickly marked the second round of appeals. Beginning within days, the process dragged once again through the system. First in the trial court; later, when the trial court denied relief on August 11, 2007, in the Pennsylvania Superior Court under Docket number 1477 WDA 2007. Finally, on July 16, 2008, the Supreme Court of Pennsylvania agreed to docket Travaglia's case by issuing an order to the Superior Court transferring jurisdiction under Capital Appeal Docket number 571 CAP.

By an alternate route, but on similar grounds, Michael Travaglia's and John Lesko's cases were once again side by side. Positioned before the highest court of the state, they will once again ask the legal scholars who compose our appellate system to weigh in, not on whether they are guilty or innocent, but instead on whether the system afforded them the underlying tenets of fairness during the past thirty years—tenets they saw fit to ignore. As always, the questions before the court are not ones of guilt or innocence, for in this case, that has been quite firmly established by the defendants' own admissions. What they are asked, as all appellate courts in this country are asked, is whether society has respected the rights of the accused in this particular case. In other words, has the system lived up to Blackstone's ratio in protecting the due process rights of the accused?

The answer, which may not come for months or even years, regardless of which way it falls, will provide very little in the way of comfort for anyone. For the victims of their rampage, there will be no last-minute stay. For the families of the victims, there will be no sense of relief (other than the fleeting sense of finality in knowing that there will be no more lengthy trials). And for the defendants, while relief may come in the knowledge that they are free to live the rest of their natural days in an eight- by eight-foot cell, it will not bring any type of true salvation; for that, if you believe in that sort of thing, must come from within.

If the Supreme Court of Pennsylvania rules in favor of the defendants in this case, there is very little likelihood that the case will end because, to the extent possible, the district attorney will most likely pursue a retrial and resentencing. If the court rules in favor of the commonwealth, it is undisputed that both Bertani and Dunham will continue their fights for their clients' rights to die in prison—of natural causes.

This process, as protective of defendants' rights as it is, has stretched over nearly three decades. It has been a lifetime for some and an eternity for others, and the only thing that is certain at this point is that in five years, there is a better chance than not that we will be discussing, in the present tense, the cases of Michael Travaglia and John Lesko.